Come Ye Children

Spurgeon's Classic in Modern English with
Fresh Insight for Families and Ministry Teams

Ryan Frank

Come Ye Children: Spurgeon's Classic in Modern English with Fresh Insight for Families and Ministry Teams
Copyright © 2025 Ryan Frank

Published by KidzMatter
432 East Val Lane, Marion, IN 46952
kidzmatter.com

Printed in the United States of America

Some portions of this book were refined with the assistance of AI technology. While aided by AI tools, this book represents the author's original work and creative expression.

Design Team:
Cover by Andrew Brooks andrewbrooks.crtv@gmail.com
Interior by Nicole Jones nicole@kidzmatter.com

ISBN Print: 978-1-968198-02-2

ISBN eBook: 978-1-968198-03-9

Dedication

To our incredible KidzMatter team—thank you for serving with excellence, creativity, and heart. Your passion for equipping leaders and reaching kids for Jesus inspires Beth and me daily. This book is as much yours as it is ours.

Table of Contents

Foreword

It's hard to put into words how much I love this incredible community of KidMin leaders. Over the years, I've had the honor of walking beside so many of you—at conferences, through our coaching groups, online gatherings, and even in quiet moments of prayer. I've laughed with you, cried with you, and stood in awe of your faithfulness. You serve with such passion, heart, and resilience. You're the ones who show up week after week, rain or shine, to tell children about Jesus. And I just want you to know this: you are seen, you are appreciated, and you are making a difference.

As a mom of three girls, children's ministry has always been personal to me. Ryan and I didn't just stumble into this work. It grew out of our love for Jesus and our deep desire to see children grow up in faith. One of our daughters was born with disabilities, which has given us a unique lens into the beauty and challenges of helping every child know they are loved by God and created for a purpose. When I look back over the years, I can say with confidence that the people who ministered to our daughters in church had some of the greatest impact on their lives—and ours.

That's why I believe so strongly in what you do. Children's ministry is not childcare. It's not just about keeping kids occupied while the adults worship. It's ministry. Eternal ministry. And it is so close to the heart of God.

Recently, a dear friend, Deborah, gave Ryan a copy of Charles Spurgeon's *Come Ye Children*. As Ryan began reading it, I could see right away how deeply it was affecting him. He would stop and read quotes out loud to me—sentences so packed with truth and conviction that they made us pause and think.

We were both amazed at how a book written over 125 years ago could speak so clearly into the realities of parenting and ministry today. Yes, the language was old-fashioned. It took a little effort to process. But the message? Unshakably clear. Charles Spurgeon understood the value of children. He understood the urgency of sharing the Gospel with them. He believed in the power of parents and teachers to help shape young hearts for eternity.

And I know that if Spurgeon were here today, he'd be cheering you on too.

That's what led Ryan to take on this project. He has poured his heart into this book. Every chapter has been carefully rewritten in modern English—not to change the meaning, but to bring clarity. His goal has always been to serve you—the parent, the teacher, the ministry leader. He wanted to make sure that this treasure of a book wasn't lost or overlooked because of outdated vocabulary. He wanted you to be able to pick it up, read it, and be refreshed.

What's even more special is that Ryan has added his own thoughts and reflections at the end of each chapter. These aren't just commentaries—they're encouragement. They're reminders that you're not alone, that what you do matters, and that the truths from Spurgeon's time are still just as relevant today.

I truly believe this book is going to bless you.

Whether you're reading it as a mom or dad, a volunteer in the nursery, a full-time children's pastor, or just someone who loves kids and wants to see them thrive—there's something here for you. I hope it stirs your heart. I hope it strengthens your calling. And I hope it reminds you that the seeds you're planting in kids' lives today will bear fruit for years to come.

As you read these pages, know that I'm in your corner. Ryan is too. More importantly, the Lord is. He sees every lesson you teach, every hug you give, every goldfish cracker you sweep up. He sees it all, and He is so pleased.

Thank you for saying yes to this calling. Thank you for loving kids well. And thank you for letting this book be part of your journey.

Beth Frank
Co-Founder of KidzMatter | Mom of 3 |
Wife of the Guy Who Rewrote This Book

Introduction

For more than thirty years, my wife Beth and I have had the incredible joy and privilege of serving the children's ministry community. What began as a passion to reach and disciple kids has grown into a lifelong calling that continues to bless us every single day. From local church ministry to national conferences, from publishing resources to walking alongside ministry leaders one-on-one, we have seen firsthand the power and beauty of ministering to children and their families. There is truly no higher calling than to help raise the next generation to know, love, and follow Jesus.

This passion led us to launch KidzMatter, a ministry devoted to equipping and encouraging the global children's ministry community. Whether you serve in a small rural church or a large urban congregation, whether you're a full-time staff member or a faithful volunteer, you matter. Your ministry matters. And KidzMatter exists to support and strengthen you as you carry out this important work. We believe that when you pour into kids, you are investing in eternity.

Not long ago, a friend gave me a special gift—a book titled *Come Ye Children* by Charles Spurgeon. Now, I'll be honest: I had never heard of it. That might surprise some of you, especially if you know how passionate I am about children's ministry. But the title was unfamiliar to me. Curious, I opened its pages and began to read.

I was blown away.

Page after page, I found timeless wisdom, deep spiritual insight, and a passionate heart for children. Spurgeon's words pierced through the years and stirred something fresh in me. His writing confirmed everything I have believed about the importance of reaching children with the Gospel. It challenged me, inspired me, and moved me to tears. I couldn't believe I had never encountered this treasure before.

And then I thought: If I've never heard of this book, I wonder how many others haven't as well?

That question was the seed that led to this project.

Before we dive into the book itself, let me tell you a little about Charles Haddon Spurgeon. Born in 1834, Spurgeon was one of the most influential preachers of the 19th century. Often called "The Prince of Preachers," he pastored the Metropolitan Tabernacle in London, where thousands gathered to hear him preach each week. His sermons were transcribed, printed, and circulated around the world. In fact, by the end of his life, it's estimated that Spurgeon had preached to over ten million people. He also founded a pastor's college, orphanages, and numerous other ministries.

But what many people don't realize is that Spurgeon had a deep and abiding love for children. He understood that children are not just the church of tomorrow—they are part of the church today. He believed that children are fully capable of understanding and responding to the Gospel, and he urged parents and teachers to take their spiritual formation seriously. His book *Come Ye Children* was a call to action, a plea for the Christian community to prioritize the evangelism and discipleship of children.

Come Ye Children was originally published in 1897, five years after Spurgeon's death. That means it was written in the style of English that was common in the late 1800s—what we often call Victorian English. While beautiful and eloquent, it can be a bit like reading Shakespeare after a long day of VBS. The sentences are long, the vocabulary is dated, and if you're anything like me, you might find yourself re-reading a sentence three times just to figure out what Spurgeon was trying to say.

Let's be honest—simple people like me need a little help translating "thou" and "thee" into "you."

That's why I decided to rewrite the book in modern-day English.

My goal was simple: I wanted to make Spurgeon's timeless message accessible to today's parents, pastors, and children's ministry leaders. I didn't want this book to gather dust on a shelf simply because the language was difficult. The truths in *Come Ye Children* are too valuable, too relevant, and too urgently needed for us to overlook.

In addition to updating the language, I've also included some personal reflections at the end of each chapter. These reflections are meant to encourage and equip you as you consider how Spurgeon's insights apply to our context today. I answer questions like: What does this mean for the parent raising kids in a digital world? How can this help the volunteer teaching preschoolers on Sunday morning? What does this look like for the ministry leader trying to build a team or cast vision for their church?

You might be surprised by how relevant this 19th-century message is to our 21st-century world.

You'll find that Spurgeon pulls no punches. He doesn't sugarcoat the importance of teaching children the Word of God. He makes it abundantly clear that the work of training up children in the faith is not optional—it's essential. And he reminds us that while parents and teachers are on the frontlines, it is ultimately God who brings the increase. Our job is to be faithful.

As you read, I hope you will be both challenged and encouraged. I hope you'll find new strength for the journey and a fresh vision for your ministry to children. I hope you'll be reminded that what you do matters deeply to the heart of God. And I hope you'll walk away with practical ideas and spiritual motivation to keep going, even when it's hard.

This book is for parents who are weary.

For teachers who wonder if they're making a difference.

For ministry leaders who need a reminder of why they started in the first place.

Beth and I are cheering you on. More importantly, the Lord is with you. He has called you to this work, and He will equip you for every step of it.

Thank you for picking up this book. Thank you for taking the time to learn from a spiritual giant like Charles Spurgeon. And thank you for investing in the lives of children. I truly believe there is no greater mission.

May this modern English edition of *Come Ye Children* be a blessing to you, just as it has been to me in preparing it for you.

Your #1 fan,
Ryan Frank

~ 1 ~

"FEED MY LAMBS"
—HOW TO DO IT

The best people in the church are not too good for this job. Don't think that just because you have other responsibilities, you shouldn't care about this holy work. Instead, be kind and willing, and help the little ones whenever you can. Encourage those whose main calling is to care for them. This message comes to all of us: "Feed My lambs." It applies to pastors and to anyone who knows the things of God. Make sure you care for the children who belong to Christ. Peter was a leader among believers, yet even he was told to feed the lambs.

Lambs are the young members of the flock. So we should give special and careful attention to those who are young in their faith. They might be older in age but still spiritual infants, needing the guidance of a good shepherd. As soon as someone comes to Christ and joins the church, they should be shown care and kindness by other believers. They're new to our community and may not have made friends among the saints yet, so we should go out of our way to befriend them. Even if we have to step away from our long-time friends for a bit, we must be extra kind to those who have just left the world behind and are now seeking safety with God and His people. Watch over these newborn believers with steady care—they are full of desire, but not much else yet. They've just come out of spiritual darkness, and their eyes are still adjusting to the light. Let's be a gentle shade for them until they can handle the brightness of the gospel day. Dedicate yourselves to the holy task of caring for the weak and discouraged. Peter himself must have felt like a brand-new recruit that morning. In a way, he had ended his public walk with Christ by denying Him and had started fresh when he "went out and cried bitterly." Now he was making a new confession of faith in front of his Lord and fellow believers, and because he could now relate to new believers, he was given the role of caring for them. Young converts are often too shy to ask for help, so our Lord brings them to our attention and commands us clearly: "Feed My lambs." This is the reward: "Whatever you did for one of the least of these, you did for Me."

No matter how young a believer is, they should openly confess their faith and be part of the flock of Christ. We're not the kind of people who doubt young faith—we see no more reason to question it in children than in those who repent later in life. In fact, we're more likely to question the latter. Fear of punishment and death often produces fake faith, while childlike faith tends to be more genuine. Think of all the things a child hasn't experienced yet that could have damaged them. Think of what they don't know—things we pray they never do. How much brightness and trust children have when they turn to God—things rarely seen in older converts! Jesus clearly cared deeply for children. Anyone who sees them as a burden or treats them like liars or fools is not much like Christ. You, the teachers in our schools, have the joyful task of discovering which children are truly part of Christ's flock. To you He says, "Feed My lambs"—in other words, teach those who are young but truly saved.

It's worth noting that the word used here for "feed My lambs" is different from the one in "feed My sheep." I won't get into the Greek, but the second "feed" means to act as a shepherd—lead, guide, organize, care for them completely. But the first "feed" is more specific—it means just to feed them, and it reminds teachers not to overlook the importance of teaching children the faith. Lambs don't need as much discipline as adults like us, who think we know so much and end up judging and competing with each other. Children mainly need to be taught the doctrines, instructions, and way of life of the gospel. They need to be shown God's truth clearly and powerfully. Why should deep doctrines—the doctrines of grace—be hidden from them? Some say these are too hard, like bones, but they're actually full of spiritual richness. And if something is too hard for a child to understand, the problem may lie with the teacher's understanding, not the child's ability— especially if the child has truly come to know God. It's our job to make truth clear. That's a big part of what we're called to do. Teach children the whole truth, and nothing but the truth, because instruction is a deep need in a child's life. A child not only has to live, like we do, but also grow. That's why they need extra nourishment. When fathers say their sons have big appetites, they should remember that we would too if we were not only running our lives but also growing while doing it. Children growing in grace need to expand in knowledge, character, action, and experience with God's power—so they especially need to be fed. They must be fed well, because if we don't feed their spiritual hunger, something else will—likely something false. Young people are easily drawn to wrong beliefs. Whether or not we teach them the truth, the devil will definitely try to teach them lies. Even with the best protection, they'll still hear falsehoods. The only way to keep their hearts from being filled with spiritual junk is to fill them with good, solid truth.

Oh, may God's Spirit help us in this work! The more young people are taught, the less likely they are to be led astray.

We're especially told to feed them because they're often forgotten. I'm afraid our sermons often go right over their heads, even though they may be just as true in their faith as older people. Blessed is the one who can speak so clearly that a child understands! Blessed is that godly woman who teaches her class in a way that fits how girls think, so the truth flows straight from her heart into theirs without anything getting in the way.

We're especially told to feed the young because it's such a worthwhile investment. No matter what we do for those saved later in life, we can only do so much. We're glad for them, of course— but at seventy, how many years of service are left, even if they live ten more? Train a child, and they might serve the Lord for fifty years. We welcome those who come into the vineyard late, but they barely pick up the tools before the sun sets and their day's work ends. The time it takes to train them often outweighs the time they have to serve. But if you take a young convert and teach them well, early faith often becomes deep faith. And deep faith, paired with many years of life ahead, means God can be glorified and people can be blessed for decades. This work is also good for us. It keeps us humble and helps us stay kind. It also strengthens our patience. If you doubt that, just try it—young Christians test our patience because we believe in them and want them to prove us right. If you want to find people with big hearts and deep compassion, look among those who work with the young. They put up with their mistakes and weaknesses—for Jesus' sake—and that work shapes them.

Reflections from Ryan

Feeding the Lambs Today

Charles Spurgeon's challenge to "Feed My lambs" hits home, doesn't it? While the language might sound a little old-fashioned, the truth is just as relevant today as it was in the 1800s. Jesus hasn't changed. Children haven't changed. And the call to love, teach, and disciple kids hasn't changed either.

If you serve in children's ministry—or you're a parent, grandparent, or caregiver—this charge is for you. Whether you lead a small group, volunteer in the nursery, pastor a church, or simply pray with your own kids at bedtime, Jesus' command is clear: Feed My lambs.

Let's break this down and get really practical. What does it look like to "feed" today's kids spiritually? And how can we live out this calling with consistency, creativity, and compassion?

1. Understand Who The Lambs Are

When Spurgeon talked about lambs, he meant two things: young people in age, and young people in faith. Some kids may have been walking with Jesus for years, while others are just beginning to ask questions. Some are churched, others aren't. Some come from stable homes, while others carry heavy burdens no child should have to carry. Some may have disabilities or special needs that affect how they learn, communicate, or experience the world. Regardless of background, ability, or circumstance—if they are young or new to faith, they are "lambs." And we're called to feed them.

You don't need a title or a degree to answer this call. You just need a heart for the next generation. The best in the church aren't too good for this work—Spurgeon made that clear. In fact, I'd argue it's one of the most important and eternally significant things any of us can do.

2. Start With Relationship

Before you can feed lambs, you have to know them. Jesus didn't say, "Throw food in their direction." He said, "Feed them"—up close and personal. This takes time and intentionality.

If you're a ministry leader, spend time getting to know the kids in your care. Learn their names. Ask about their hobbies. Show up at their sports games or school plays. If you're a parent, carve out one-on-one time that goes beyond routines. Sit down and ask spiritual questions. Listen—really listen—to their hearts.

Kids may not remember every Bible lesson you teach, but they will remember the adult who made them feel seen, heard, and loved.

3. Feed Them The Truth

Spurgeon pushed back on the idea that kids can't handle deep theology. He reminded us that truth isn't just for grown-ups—it's for everyone. And I agree. Kids are sponges. They're wired to learn. So let's not water down the gospel. Let's give them solid food—yes, in kid-sized bites—but with all the rich flavor of God's truth.

Don't shy away from teaching kids about grace, forgiveness, sin, the cross, or the power of the Holy Spirit. Use stories, object lessons, and illustrations that make these concepts real—but don't skip over them. Kids can understand big ideas when they're taught well. In fact, I've seen many kids explain the gospel more clearly than some adults.

Keep it simple, but never shallow.

4. Protect Their Diet

We live in a world that is aggressively feeding children spiritual junk food. From entertainment to social media, from the classroom to their peers, kids are being bombarded with messages that shape their worldview.

That's why your role is so important. If you're not feeding them truth, someone else is feeding them lies. The enemy is strategic—and he's not waiting until kids are 18 to start his attacks.

You don't have to be paranoid, but you do need to be proactive. Monitor what kids are watching, listening to, and engaging with. Create a home or classroom culture where biblical truth is the foundation. Ask questions like, "What do you think God says about that?" or "Let's see what the Bible says together."

We can't control everything our kids encounter—but we can fill them up so full of truth that there's no room left for garbage.

5. Include the Kids

One of the most beautiful things about Jesus' ministry is how He constantly welcomed children. He didn't see them as a nuisance or a distraction. He saw them as essential to the Kingdom. Sadly, in too many churches today, children are seen as the "future of the church" instead of the present.

We need to change that mindset.

Let kids serve. Let them worship. Let them ask questions. Let them help lead games or greet guests or pray out loud. Let them participate in real ministry. Because when we treat them like full members of the body of Christ, they begin to see themselves that way too.

6. Invest Long-Term

Spurgeon reminded us that time spent pouring into children often pays off for decades. I've seen it over and over again: a child who was faithfully discipled at 8 or 10 grows into a young adult who leads worship, preaches, starts a ministry, or serves overseas. You may not see the fruit right away, but your investment matters.

That child in your class with the short attention span? He could become a pastor. That little girl with a heart for helping others? She might be the next Christian influencer, author, or counselor. Don't underestimate what God can do through a young life, especially one that's been well-fed.

7. Let It Shape You

Finally, don't forget that feeding lambs doesn't just grow them—it grows you too. It teaches humility, stretches your patience, and deepens your dependence on God. Kids will test your limits, ask hard questions, and sometimes make you want to pull your hair out. But they'll also surprise you with their insight, encourage you with their honesty, and bless you with their love.

If you want to become more like Jesus, spend time with children. That's where His heart is. That's where real ministry happens.

Final Thoughts

So let me close with this encouragement: Don't wait for someone else to do this work. Don't assume the children's pastor or church staff has it covered. If you know Jesus, if you love kids, and if you're willing to serve, then this calling is for you.

"Feed My lambs."

It's not just a suggestion. It's a command straight from the heart of the Savior.

Let's say yes.

~ 2 ~

Do Not Hinder the Children

When it comes to keeping children away from Jesus, let's take a close look at how it plays out. One of the sad results of this mindset is that often there's nothing in the church service designed for children. The sermon goes over their heads, and the preacher doesn't consider that a problem—he might even be proud of it. Not long ago, someone—trying, I think, to make me feel small—wrote to tell me he had met some Black folks who had read my sermons and really enjoyed them. He added that he believed my sermons were perfect for "those kinds of people." Yes, my preaching was, according to him, just the sort of stuff for "those folks." What he didn't realize was that his comment brought me real joy. If my preaching connects with working-class people, with housemaids, with children—then I know it can reach anyone. I consider it a great honor to preach to "those kinds of people," if by that he means the poor, the overlooked, the rough and ragged. I think there's nothing greater than winning the hearts of every-day people. The same applies to children. People sometimes say about someone, "He's only good for teaching kids—not really a preacher." But I'll tell you this: in God's eyes, anyone who doesn't care about children isn't really a preacher at all. Every sermon and service should include at least something for the little ones. It's a mistake to forget that.

Parents fall into the same trap when they leave faith out of their child's education. Some parents think their kids can't really be saved while they're still young, so they don't consider it very important where they send them to school. But that's wrong. Many parents even overlook this when their sons and daughters are finishing up school. They send them off to other countries, to places full of spiritual and moral dangers, thinking this will help complete their "well-rounded" education. I've seen the outcome far too often—young men who come back as full-blown rebels, and young women who return shallow and flirtatious. You reap what you sow. Let's expect our children to know the Lord. Let's start early—teach them the name of Jesus alongside their ABCs. Let them read their first lessons from the Bible. It's remarkable how quickly kids learn to read using the New Testament. There's a special power in that book that captures the hearts of children. So let's never be guilty, as parents, of ignoring their spiritual training. If we do, we might be responsible for the eternal loss of their souls.

Another result of this attitude is that many churches don't expect children to be saved while they're still young. They figure it's enough to teach them values that might help them later in life. But the idea of children being saved now—as children—and being treated as real believers, just like adults, is considered ridiculous by some. But that so-called "ridiculous" idea is one I hold onto with all my heart. I believe the kingdom of God belongs to children—here and in heaven.

Another sad outcome is that many people just don't believe in child conversions. Some are always skeptical when they hear about a child being saved—they sharpen their words like knives, ready to take a bite. Now, they're right to insist that children should be thoughtfully examined before being baptized and welcomed into the church. But they're wrong to think that children should only be accepted in rare cases. I agree that we need to be careful—but that applies to everyone, not just kids. We should use the same standard across the board.

How often do adults expect boys and girls to act as serious and composed as grown-ups? Truth be told, we'd all be better off if we never stopped being kids—if we added adult virtues to childlike qualities. Why should we think that a child must instantly become twenty years older the moment they're saved? I remember a very serious person once calling me off the playground after I had joined the church. He scolded me for playing games like bat and ball with the boys. "How can you play like that if you're a child of God?" he asked. I explained that I was working as an assistant teacher, and part of my job was to play with the boys. That explanation changed his view—but it was clear he believed a saved boy shouldn't ever play.

Don't others sometimes expect more perfect behavior from children than they expect from themselves? If a godly child loses their temper or forgets something small, they're often condemned as a little hypocrite—even by adults who are far from perfect themselves. But Jesus warned us, "Be careful that you don't look down on one of these little ones." Don't speak unkindly of your younger brothers and sisters in Christ. Jesus treasures His lambs so much that He carries them close to His heart. And I urge you, if you follow the Lord, to show that same gentleness to His little ones.

"They brought young children to Him so He could touch them, but the disciples scolded those who brought them. When Jesus saw it, He was deeply upset." He didn't get upset very often—certainly not deeply upset. So this must have been serious. Jesus was upset because the disciples were doing the exact opposite of what He wanted. They wronged the mothers by rebuking them for doing something motherly—something Jesus actually appreciated. These women brought their children out of love and respect for Jesus. They wanted a blessing from Him more than money. They hoped that Jesus' touch would bring their children joy and favor. Even if their expectations weren't perfect, Jesus saw the heart behind it. He was very upset that these devoted mothers were being turned away.

And the disciples wronged the children too. Sweet little ones— what had they done to deserve rejection? They weren't trying to be disruptive. Those dear kids would have gladly fallen at His feet in love for the Teacher who spoke with such kindness. Why scold them? They meant no harm.

Even worse, they wronged Jesus Himself. They made Him look cold and distant, like the arrogant religious leaders. If people had thought Jesus didn't care about children, they would have misunderstood His heart completely. His heart is a wide-open harbor where many small boats are welcome. Jesus, the childlike Savior, felt completely at home with kids. The holy child Jesus had a deep connection with them. Could He really be represented by His own followers as someone who shuts children out? That would be a terrible distortion of who He is. That's why Jesus was deeply grieved. It hurt Him to see mothers disrespected, children rejected, and His own character misrepresented. When we do anything that keeps a child from Jesus, it deeply upsets Him. He says, "Step aside. Don't get in the way. Let them come to Me. Do not hold them back."

It also went against what He taught. He said, "Unless you receive the kingdom of God like a little child, you'll never enter it." Jesus didn't teach that we need to reach a certain age or earn our way into grace. In fact, He taught the opposite—we need to become smaller, more humble, less full of ourselves. The more we empty ourselves, the more room there is for His grace. Think you'll reach Jesus by climbing the ladder of knowledge? Come down—you'll meet Him at the bottom. Think you'll reach Him by gaining years of experience? Come down—He stands on level ground. "When I'm older, I'll be ready for Christ," you say. No—stay right where you are. Jesus meets you at the entrance of life. You are never more ready than now. He asks for nothing but your emptiness—so that He can be everything for you. That's His message. So when we turn children away for not meeting some standard, we go directly against the gospel of God's grace.

Finally, it went against what Jesus actually did. He proved this by His actions: "He took them in His arms, put His hands on them, and blessed them." His whole life shows no hint of rejection. He said, "Whoever comes to Me I will never turn away." If He had refused children for being too young, that statement would no longer be true—but it is always true. He welcomes anyone who comes to Him. Scripture says, "This man receives sinners and eats with them." If you wanted to draw a picture of Jesus, draw a shepherd holding a lamb close to his chest—not a harsh shepherd sending dogs after the lambs to chase them and their mothers away.

Reflections from Ryan

"Let the Children Come"

Charles Spurgeon's words hit deep in this chapter—and they still ring true nearly 125+ years later. He reminds us that one of the greatest dangers in the church is not open opposition to children, but quiet neglect. We don't often slam the door in their faces; we just forget to open it wide.

I've been in children's ministry most of my life. I've met many lead pastors who believe the most important part of Sunday is the message they deliver from the pulpit. I've seen churches spend thousands of dollars on LED walls while budgeting very little for their nursery. And I've met parents who pour everything into their child's sports or academics—yet when it comes to faith, it's on the back burner: "until they're older."

Friends, this must not be so.

Jesus was deeply displeased when His disciples tried to keep the kids away. That's a strong reaction from the Son of God. He didn't say, "They'll come around eventually" or "Let's wait until they're more mature." No—He was grieved that anyone would block their path.

So how do we bring this into our world today?

Let me speak first to parents.

1. Your Child's Faith Can Be Real—Right Now

One of the greatest lies Christian parents believe is that their child will "get serious about God when they're older." No. Jesus is ready for them now. Spurgeon said, "Let us expect our children to know the Lord." That's a mindset shift. We don't hope it might happen one day—we believe it can happen today.

- Do you pray with your child like you expect them to connect with God?
- Do you talk about Jesus at home like He's their Savior, not just yours?
- Do you open the Bible with them—not just to teach them, but to walk alongside them as disciples?

When you expect your child's faith to be real, you stop treating Christianity as a future add-on and start discipling them as a present reality.

2. Don't Outsource Their Spiritual Growth

I love Sunday school. I love children's church. I've spent most of my life building those environments. But no amount of programming can replace the influence of a parent who walks with Jesus.

Deuteronomy 6 reminds us that teaching our children the ways of God is an all-day mission: "When you sit at home, when you walk along the road, when you lie down and when you get up." That's daily life. That's real discipleship. That's where faith gets planted deep.

Spurgeon said, "Let us mingle the name of Jesus with their ABCs." In other words, make Jesus the background music of your home. Not in a fake or forced way—but in a natural, life-giving way that helps your kids see that God is not a Sunday morning add-on. He is the center of it all.

Now, let me speak to children's ministry leaders.

3. Build Ministry Environments With Children In Mind

Too often, church programming is built for adults and then retrofitted for kids. Spurgeon criticized sermons that "go over children's heads," and I think the same can be said of much of our church culture. Do the songs we sing make sense to a 7-year-old? Are we preaching in ways a 10-year-old can grasp? Are our environments physically, emotionally, and cognitively welcoming to all children—including those with disabilities or special needs?

I'm not saying we need to water anything down. In fact, I believe children can handle more depth than we often assume. But let's teach truth in ways that truly connect—with stories, visuals, hands-on examples, and language that speaks to where each child is, not just where we expect the average child to be.

Some kids may need more time to process. Others may need visual supports, a quiet space, or extra patience from a volunteer. And all of them need to know they are seen, valued, and included.

Jesus didn't adjust the message for kids, but He always adjusted the approach. He got down on their level. He blessed them. He welcomed them close.

We should do the same. Every child, every ability, every time.

4. Take Young Faith Seriously

Spurgeon called out the way some church leaders roll their eyes at kids who claim to follow Jesus. It still happens today. I've seen children excited about their faith—only to be met with suspicion. "We'll see if it lasts." "Let's wait a few years before we take this too seriously."

Meanwhile, we cheer for a 9-year-old who scores a basket but question her when she says she wants to get baptized.

If Jesus welcomes children, we must also believe they can genuinely repent, believe, and follow Him. Yes, we should ask questions. Yes, we should make sure they understand. But let's do it with hope, not hesitation.

Their faith may not look exactly like an adult's—and that's okay. Don't expect them to become 25 overnight. Let them be kids. Let them love Jesus in their own childlike way.

5. Protect Them—But Don't Shelter Them From God's Presence

In Spurgeon's day, some parents sent their kids away to Europe for education—completely overlooking the spiritual cost. Today, it's not much different. We fill our kids' schedules with practices, parties, and pressures, and then wonder why their spiritual lives are so shallow.

I'm not saying you shouldn't aim for academic or social excellence. But I am saying that if our kids grow up with every opportunity in the world and never learn to walk with Jesus, we've failed them.

As Spurgeon said so powerfully, "We may be guilty of the blood of their souls."

That's sobering.

So as parents and pastors, as leaders and caregivers, let's hear the cry of Jesus again: "Let the little children come to Me, and do not hinder them."

6. Remove Every Obstacle

This is our mission. Clear the path. Remove distractions. Break down walls. If there's anything in your ministry that says, "Wait until you're older," remove it.

Make it easy for children to come to Jesus.

Let them come with noise and joy.

Let them come with questions and messes.

Let them come with simple faith and honest hearts.

And when they come, don't stand back and evaluate—celebrate.

Final Thoughts

You may think your children's ministry doesn't matter as much as "big church." You may feel like wiping noses, prepping crafts, or holding crying babies is a small thing.

But to Jesus, it's not small.

He sees. He cares. He is deeply pleased when we open the door wide to the children.

Let them come. And let's lead them well.

~ 3 ~

THE DISCIPLES AND THE MOTHERS

The close disciples of our Lord were a truly honorable group of men; even with their mistakes and shortcomings, they must have been deeply shaped by being near someone so perfect and full of love. So, if these men—who were the best of the best—rebuked the mothers who brought their young children to Jesus, it must be a fairly common mistake in the church. I'm afraid this cold attitude still shows up almost everywhere. I don't want to be unkind, but if we each did a little self-examination, we might discover that we're guilty here too—and, like Pharaoh's butler, we'd say, "I remember my mistakes today." Have we focused on reaching children with the Gospel as much as we have adults? What's that? You think I'm being sarcastic? Do you make any effort to lead anyone to Christ? What more can I say? It's a sad thing when a Christian has Cain's attitude, saying, "Am I my brother's keeper?" It's tragic when we feed ourselves spiritually while letting the spiritually starving die. But let me ask you—if you did care about souls, wouldn't you still think starting with kids was too ordinary, too basic? Sadly, many do. It's a widespread problem.

I believe the disciples' attitude came from a misguided zeal for Jesus. These men probably thought that bringing children to the Savior would just get in the way. He had more important things to do—He had just silenced the Pharisees, taught crowds of people, and healed the sick. Surely it wasn't appropriate to bother Him with children! The kids wouldn't understand His teaching, and they didn't need to be healed—so why bring them? They might interrupt something important. So the disciples were basically saying, "Take your children home, ladies. Teach them the Law yourselves, read the Psalms and the Prophets to them, and pray with them there. Jesus can't lay hands on every child. If we let these in, the whole neighborhood will show up and distract Him from His real mission. Can't you see that? Why are you being so thoughtless?" They respected Jesus so much that they didn't want Him to be seen as just a teacher for little kids. It might've been well-meaning, but it was misguided. Even today, some Christians hesitate to welcome too many children into the church, as if it might become "just a Sunday school." I remember when a woman with a scandalous past was saved in one of our towns, and some Christians objected to her joining the church. Some ungodly people even posted public signs saying the Baptist pastor had baptized a prostitute. I told my friend to take it as an honor. In the same way, if anyone criticizes us for welcoming children into the church, let's wear that as a badge of honor. Holy children can't hurt us. God will give us enough mature believers to guide the church wisely. We won't accept anyone into the church without signs of real spiritual life—no matter how old they are. But we also won't reject any real believers, no matter how young. We don't look down on our cautious brothers and sisters, but we do wish they'd be more cautious in areas where it's really needed. Jesus will never be dishonored by the presence of children—we should be more concerned about the adults.

Part of the disciples' mistake was not recognizing that even healthy, happy children need Jesus. If one of those mothers had said, "My child is possessed by an evil spirit—I have to bring him to Jesus," Peter or James or John would've jumped in to help. Or if another mom had said, "My daughter is wasting away from a disease. Please let me bring her to the Master to be healed," the disciples would have said, "Make way for her!" But these cheerful little ones with bright eyes and chattering voices—why bring them to Jesus? The disciples forgot that even healthy, innocent-looking children deeply need the Savior's grace. If you start believing the modern idea that your kids don't need to be saved—that just because they're born into a Christian home, they're better off and just need to be "nurtured"—then you've lost one of the biggest reasons to pray for them. Believe me, your children need the Holy Spirit to give them new hearts and a right spirit. Otherwise, they'll go the wrong way just like all other kids. No matter how young, there's still a heart of stone inside them—and that stone must be replaced or it will ruin them. Even when sin hasn't yet shown itself, the tendency to sin is already there. That sinful nature can only be overcome by the power of the Holy Spirit making them new. I wish the church would stop clinging to the old Jewish idea that physical birth gives someone spiritual privilege. Even in the Old Testament, there were signs that the true children of God weren't born by bloodline but by God's choice—just look at Ishmael and Isaac, or Esau and Jacob. Doesn't the church know what Jesus said: "That which is born of the flesh is flesh; that which is born of the Spirit is spirit"? "Who can bring something pure from something impure?" Being born physically brings human weakness, but it can't bring spiritual life. In the New Covenant, we're told clearly that God's children are "born not of blood, nor of human effort, nor of human desire, but born of God." In the Old Covenant, physical birth brought some advantages. But to be part of the Covenant of Grace, you must be born again. Your first birth makes you part of Adam's family. You need a second birth to belong to Christ.

"But," someone says, "doesn't the Bible say, 'The promise is to you and your children'?" That verse has been misused more than almost any other. I've heard it twisted to support teachings that are far from what it actually says. If you only quote half a sentence and leave the rest out, you can make someone sound like they meant the exact opposite of what they said. What does the full verse say? Acts 2:39—"The promise is to you and your children, and to all who are far away, everyone whom the Lord our God calls to Himself." That's a beautifully wide invitation. It's the basis for the call: "Repent and be baptized, every one of you." It's not a special privilege passed down to a select few. It's grace offered equally—to your children, to outsiders, and to all whom God calls. Nowhere in the New Testament does it say that grace is passed down by family line. It comes to those whom God calls, whether their parents are saints or sinners. It's outrageous to quote only half a verse to make it say what it clearly does not mean. You must look at your children through biblical eyes—as born in sin, shaped in iniquity, and under judgment just like everyone else. Even if you come from a long line of faithful ministers and godly people, your children are still born with the same need to be rescued by Jesus and renewed by the Holy Spirit. Yes, they are blessed to grow up hearing the gospel, but their spiritual need is the same as anyone else's. When you understand this, you'll see why your children should be brought to Jesus as soon as possible—carried in the arms of your prayers and your faith to the only One who can save them.

I've sometimes seen deeper spiritual understanding in 10- or 12-year-olds than in people who are 50 or 60. It's an old saying that some children are "born with beards." Some boys are like little grown-ups, and some girls are wise beyond their years. Age doesn't always measure maturity. I knew a boy who, by the time he was fifteen, had older Christians saying, "That boy's got the heart of a 60-year-old—he understands spiritual things so deeply." And it was true. That young man had a greater grasp of God's truth than anyone around him, no matter their age. I don't know why, but it's a fact: some kids are spiritually old, and some adults are still immature. Don't say kids can't repent! I've known children who cried themselves to sleep night after night, feeling the weight of their sin. If you want to understand the fear of God's judgment, I can tell you what I felt as a boy—it was awful. If you want to know joy in Jesus, children can be full of it. If you want to see real faith in Christ, don't look to adults confused by the nonsense of modern teachings. Look at a child who simply trusts Jesus, loves Him, and knows with certainty that they are saved. Children are often more ready to believe than adults. As we age, we tend to become less able to believe—our hearts grow harder, more cynical, and further from God. A child's heart is like fresh soil—soft, open, not yet hardened by pride, greed, or worldly thinking. And ultimately, the new birth is the work of the Holy Spirit, and He can work just as easily in a child's heart as in an adult's.

Others have kept children away simply because they forget how valuable they are. A soul's worth doesn't depend on how old it is. "Oh, it's just a child." "Kids are annoying." "They're always underfoot." You hear people say things like that. May God forgive those who despise little ones! You might not like this, but I'll say it anyway—a child is worth more than an old man. It's amazing grace when God saves a 70-year-old, but how much time does that person have left to serve Him? At 50 or 60, most of our strength is gone. If we spent our youth serving sin, there's not much left to offer God. But a child—there's still so much potential! If they give their life to Christ early, they can live a whole life of joyful, faithful service. Who knows how God might use them? Entire nations might hear the gospel because of one saved child. A famous schoolteacher used to take off his hat to his students, just in case one might grow up to be Prime Minister. How much more should we honor a saved child? We don't know how brightly they might shine or how soon they might be in heaven. Let's value children the way God does. Let's not hold them back—we should be eager to lead them to Jesus right now.

The more spiritually mature we are, and the more childlike our own hearts become, the more at home we'll be with children. We'll understand their fears and hopes, their budding faith and growing love. Being around young believers will feel like walking through a garden in full bloom, or a vineyard where the first grapes are giving off a sweet smell.

Reflections from Ryan

Welcoming Children Like Jesus Did

As I sit with Spurgeon's words in Chapter 3, one truth rings loud and clear: Children matter to Jesus. And because they matter to Him, they must matter to us.

This chapter reminds me that even the best-intentioned leaders can overlook the importance of children in the church. The disciples weren't trying to be cruel. They thought they were protecting Jesus, helping Him focus on "bigger" things. But in their effort to honor Him, they missed His heart entirely.

If you're in children's ministry—whether full-time, part-time, or as a faithful volunteer—I want to encourage you today: Don't let anyone (including yourself!) convince you that working with children is second-tier ministry. Spurgeon draws attention to a problem that still exists today: too many church leaders and members see children's ministry as "childcare" instead of "Kingdom work."

I've seen it up close. I've been in meetings where we're mapping out the church's vision, and children get mentioned as an afterthought. I've walked into churches where the kids are tucked away in a basement or in the back hall, far removed from the heart of the church's life.

Friend, if we wait until children are old enough to fully understand before we engage their hearts, we've waited too long.

Let me be clear: Jesus didn't wait. He welcomed the children when others wanted to send them away. He laid His hands on them. He blessed them. He gave them time, attention, and love.

And we are called to do the same.

1. The Church Is Not a Waiting Room

One of the biggest takeaways from this chapter is that children don't have to wait until they're older to meet Jesus. The church isn't a waiting room for spiritual maturity—it's a training ground. And that training starts early.

As leaders and parents, we must shift our mindset. We often invest our best energy in adult ministries, assuming that's where the most "impact" is. But what if the greatest spiritual harvest is right in front of us—in the form of wiggly five-year-olds and wide-eyed third graders?

I've often said: You don't have to wait until they're grown to lead them toward spiritual growth. Kids can understand the gospel. They can experience the Holy Spirit. They can live for Jesus, even when they're still learning to tie their shoes.

We've got to stop saying, "They're too young" and start saying, "Let's plant seeds now." The sooner a child hears the gospel, sees it lived out, and experiences the love of Christ through His people, the better.

Every Child Needs a New Heart

Spurgeon is blunt—and rightly so—about a dangerous mindset that sneaks into many Christian homes. He warns against the belief that children born to Christian parents are naturally "better off" spiritually. I know it's easy to assume that because we raise our kids in church, pray with them at meals, and teach them Bible stories, they're fine. But the truth is: every child needs a Savior.

Our kids are not saved by proximity. They're not born into the Kingdom of God just because they're born into a Christian home. They must be born again.

That's not a message of fear—it's a call to urgency and intentionality.

Parents: lead your kids to Jesus—not just in theory, but in practice. Pray with them. Talk about sin and grace. Help them understand repentance and faith. Celebrate when they make a decision to follow Jesus, but keep walking with them in discipleship every day after that.

Children's ministry leaders: never underestimate the importance of your work. Every story you teach, every prayer you pray, every silly game that opens the door to a serious conversation—it all matters.

You're not just "watching the kids." You're helping rescue souls. You're shaping future missionaries, pastors, moms, dads, doctors, and world-changers.

2. We Must Repent of Low Expectations

Another striking truth in this chapter is the reminder that children are capable of deep spiritual understanding—even more so, sometimes, than adults.

As someone who's spent years working with kids, I've seen it first-hand. I've seen an eight-year-old explain the gospel more clearly than some adults. I've heard a ten-year-old pray with more passion and sincerity than seasoned believers. I've watched children worship with tears in their eyes and joy in their hearts.

Children are not spiritually inferior. Their faith may be simple, but simple doesn't mean shallow. In fact, simple faith often reflects a deeper trust.

Adults tend to complicate faith—we analyze, doubt, reason our way out of believing. Kids, on the other hand, often take Jesus at His word. And isn't that exactly what He wants?

If you lead in children's ministry, raise the bar. Expect more. Challenge kids to read the Bible for themselves. Invite them into meaningful prayer. Give them leadership opportunities. Encourage them to serve. Don't wait until they're 16 to teach them spiritual disciplines. Start now.

3. Don't Miss the Value of a Child

Spurgeon makes a bold statement here—one I've thought about often. He says a boy is "more worth saving" than a man. That might sound shocking at first, but when you really think about it, it makes perfect sense.

Saving a child means redeeming not just a soul, but a future. It's the opportunity to help them live their entire life for Christ—not just what's left. It's giving them time to grow in faith, develop their calling, and impact the world around them for decades to come.

And this includes every child. The ones who are loud. The ones who are quiet. The ones who catch on quickly, and the ones who need more time and care. It includes children with disabilities or special needs— kids who may not learn or communicate like others, but who carry just as much value, purpose, and potential in God's Kingdom. Their futures matter just as much, and their lives can be just as powerfully used by God.

What if the child in your ministry today is the one who leads thousands to Christ tomorrow? What if that quiet girl on the back row is the next Corrie ten Boom or Beth Moore? What if that kid who never seems to sit still is a future pastor, evangelist, or missionary? And what if that child with special needs becomes a powerful witness of God's grace through their faith, resilience, and story?

Let's stop seeing children as "in the way" and start seeing them as "on the way"—on the way to being used by God in mighty and meaningful ways.

4. Let's Lead Like Jesus

In the end, this chapter calls us to lead like Jesus—welcoming, blessing, and valuing children. That means we must create churches, ministries, and homes where kids feel seen, heard, and loved.

And it also means we must reject the subtle lies that tell us:

- "They're too young."
- "They'll understand later."
- "Let's focus on the adults first."

Jesus didn't see children as a distraction. He saw them as a priority. And so should we.

Let's raise a generation of leaders, parents, and pastors who believe in kids. Who invest in kids. Who fight for kids. Who disciple kids like Jesus did—lovingly, intentionally, and urgently.

Thank you for what you do. Thank you for your commitment to kids, even when it's hard, messy, or unnoticed.

Keep welcoming the children. Jesus is still saying, "Let them come to Me."

~ 4 ~

THE CHILDREN'S SHEPHERD

Simon Peter wasn't a Welshman, but he had a lot of what we might call "Welsh passion" in him. He was exactly the kind of person who could grab the attention of kids. Children love to gather around warmth—whether it comes from a fireplace or from a person's heart. Some people just seem cold as ice, and kids naturally stay away from them. Church classes and Sunday schools tend to shrink when someone like that is in charge. But when a man or woman has a warm, kind heart, children are drawn to them like flies to a sunny wall in autumn. That's why Jesus says to warm-hearted Simon, "Feed My lambs." He's the right person for the job.

Simon Peter was also a man with deep life experience. He knew what it meant to fail. He had felt deep conviction. He had sinned greatly and had been greatly forgiven. Now, he had grown into a gentle humility and openly confessed how beautiful and loving Jesus was. We need men and women like that to talk to new believers—especially children. They need to hear what the Lord has done in our lives—our failures, our struggles, and how God has helped us. Young people want to hear from someone who has walked the road ahead of them. I'd say that mature believers carry wisdom on their lips. When shared with love, their life stories can nourish and grow young faith.

Simon Peter was also deeply grateful. He owed everything to Jesus. According to the Kingdom's rule, "The one who is forgiven much, loves much." If you've never taken up the work of serving Christ, but you could do it well, now's the time to step forward and say, "I've left this to others long enough. I still have passion in my heart and wisdom to share. I'm going to join those who are faithfully feeding the lambs in Jesus' name." That's who Jesus calls to this work.

And when the Lord calls someone to a job, He also prepares them for it. How was Peter prepared to feed Christ's lambs? First, by being fed himself. Jesus gave him breakfast before giving him his commission. You can't feed others—kids or adults—if you're spiritually starving. It's great to serve all day Sunday, but it's unwise to skip hearing the gospel yourself. First, be nourished—then nourish others.

Even more importantly, Peter was prepared by spending time with Jesus. He would never forget that morning—the voice, the look that cut straight to his heart, the very air around the risen Lord. That time with Jesus shaped Peter's heart and tuned his voice to go and feed the lambs. I encourage you to read helpful books—but more than anything, spend time with Jesus. Let Him be your greatest teacher. Get close to Him. One hour of being in His presence is better preparation for teaching than anything else—whether you're working with kids or adults.

Peter was also prepared in a tougher way—through self-examination. Jesus asked him three times, "Simon, son of John, do you love Me?" Over and over again, that question challenged him. Before God can use us to offer living water to others, we often need to be cleaned up inside. Honest self-examination never hurts some-one who truly loves Jesus. It's the fake believers who fear being exposed or challenged. But the genuine ones want to be sure they really love the Lord, so they examine their hearts, ask tough questions, and allow the Spirit to search them.

And that self-examination should especially focus on our love—because love is the most important preparation for feeding Christ's lambs. We must love both Jesus and the children. Like Aaron, we must carry their names on our hearts. Without love, teaching becomes empty. It's like a blacksmith without fire or a builder without mortar. A shepherd who doesn't love his sheep is just a hired hand—he'll run when danger comes and abandon the flock. Where there's no love, there's no life. Living lambs can't be fed by dead hearts. We teach love. Our whole message is about God's love in Christ. So how can we teach love if we don't have it ourselves? Our goal is to spark love in the hearts of our listeners—but how can we light a flame if we're soaking wet with worldliness and indifference? Instead of sparking warmth, we might smother their spirits. These children live in Christ's love—shouldn't they also live in ours? Jesus calls them "My lambs," and they are—so let's love them for His sake. They were chosen in love, redeemed in love, called in love, cleansed in love, and they'll be carried all the way to heaven by love. You and I won't fit into God's big plan of love unless our hearts are full of it. Love is the highest qualification for ministry—whether it's preaching in church or teaching a Sunday school class. If you love, then feed. If you don't, wait for God to stir your heart—don't step into sacred work with a cold spirit.

When it comes to the weakest in the flock—new believers and children—our main job is to feed. Every sermon, every lesson should provide spiritual nourishment. It's not enough to shout, "Believe! Believe!" when no one understands what to believe.

Tambourines and gimmicks won't feed the soul. Children need clear, solid gospel truth. If you've got meat to serve, then ring the dinner bell—but a bell won't fill anyone's stomach if there's no food on the table. Getting kids to show up on Sunday is pointless if we don't give them real, life-changing truth. Feed the lambs. You don't need to entertain them with bells and ribbons—just feed them.

Feeding lambs is quiet, humble work. Do you know any shepherds by name? Probably not. They don't get their names in newspapers or honored by politicians. They work behind the scenes. You wouldn't know a shepherd from a farmer or a delivery guy—he works quietly, day and night, especially in spring when lambs are born. Year after year, he keeps going without fanfare or awards. It's the same with many faithful children's teachers— you rarely hear their names, but they're doing Kingdom work that future generations will thank them for. The Lord sees them, and we'll hear their names in eternity—maybe not before.

Feeding lambs takes care. You can't feed them just anything— especially Christ's lambs. Young believers are vulnerable, and poor teaching can do real harm. Children are quick to believe things, even dangerous things, so we must be very careful what we teach. If adults need to be cautious about what they hear, how much more should we be cautious about what we say. Every child is different. Feeding them means knowing what each one needs and teaching them accordingly.

It's also ongoing work. "Feed My lambs" isn't a one-time job— it's lifelong. You can't feed lambs once a week and expect them to survive. They'll starve between Sundays. Good teachers check in throughout the week, pray for their kids, and live lives that show Jesus even when they aren't teaching. Shepherding lambs is daily, hourly work. Ask any shepherd—he'll tell you that during lambing season, he's never off duty. He catches short naps here and there, always on alert. It's the same with those who feed Christ's lambs—they don't rest until the kids are saved and growing in holiness.

It's hard work, too. Anyone who avoids the hard work of ministry will have a lot to answer for one day. Think ministry is easy? The one who treats it lightly will find it very heavy at the end. Nothing drains a person more than truly caring for souls. Teachers know this too—you can't help others grow without pouring yourself out. You have to study. You have to come prepared with something fresh and true. I'm sure you often wonder how you'll get through the next Sunday—and if you're doing it right, that pressure is real. You can't just show up unprepared and give God your leftovers. It takes real effort to present the gospel in a way that little ones can understand and receive.

And all of this must be done in a very special spirit. A true shepherd has a unique blend of graces. He's full of passion—but not easily angered. He's gentle—but he leads with authority. He's loving—but he doesn't overlook sin. He influences children without being harsh. He's cheerful—but not silly. He's free—but not careless. He's serious—but not gloomy. If you're going to care for lambs, you must have the heart of a lamb. And thank God, there's a Lamb on the throne who cares for us—He understands us because He became like us. The shepherd's heart is a rare and priceless gift. A truly effective pastor or teacher has certain qualities that set them apart. Think of a bird sitting on her eggs or feeding her young—while others fly freely, she gives her whole life to nurturing her little ones. That same kind of passion fills the heart of a true soul-winner. He would die to see souls saved. He works, pleads, and sacrifices because his heart is full of love. If only they could be saved, he would give anything—even his own heaven. Like Paul, he sometimes feels he'd trade everything if it would bring others to Christ. Most people won't understand that level of passion—but may the Holy Spirit awaken it in us. Then we'll truly be shepherds to the lambs.

This is the work: "Feed My lambs."

Reflections from Ryan

Feeding the Lambs Today

When I read Spurgeon's words, "Feed My lambs," I hear the voice of Jesus not just speaking to Simon Peter, but calling each of us who lead, teach, parent, and serve the next generation. Whether you're a full-time children's pastor, a volunteer teacher, or a mom or dad tucking your child into bed—this chapter reminds us: your work matters. The lambs need feeding.

1. "Feed My Lambs" Is Still The Call Today

Let's face it—children's ministry today looks a lot different than it did in Spurgeon's day. We've got screens in every pocket, busy schedules, and a generation growing up in a world that's more distracted, divided, and digitally saturated than ever before. But guess what? The basic needs of a child's soul haven't changed. Kids still need truth. They still need love. They still need Jesus. And they still need someone to feed them.

2. You Can't Pour Out What Hasn't Been Poured In

Spurgeon emphasizes that the first requirement for feeding others is being fed yourself. That hits home. Too many leaders today are running on empty. We're preparing lessons, organizing events, managing volunteers—but we're spiritually starving. You can't pour out what hasn't been poured in. Jesus gave Peter breakfast before giving him a mission. In the same way, we need to prioritize our own time with the Lord. Not just so we can be better leaders—but because we're His children too. Quiet time in the Word, prayer, worship, even taking a Sabbath—these are not luxuries for the Christian leader. They are survival tools.

He also points out that Peter was a man with experience—a man who had failed, been forgiven, and grown humble. That's encouraging, isn't it? You don't have to be perfect to be used by God. In fact, it's your story—your struggles, your scars, your victories—that will often connect with the hearts of children more than a perfectly prepared lesson. Parents, your kids need to hear how God is working in your life. Leaders, your honesty creates space for transformation. Let's not be afraid to share our testimonies, especially with young ears and tender hearts. They may not remember every Bible verse you quote, but they'll never forget how your eyes lit up when you talked about what Jesus did for you.

3. Love Is Not Optional—It's Foundational

One of my favorite parts of this chapter is Spurgeon's emphasis on love. If you don't love the kids, don't teach them. That's a bold statement, but a necessary one. Love isn't optional—it's foundational. Without love, teaching becomes dry and mechanical. With love, it becomes life-giving. The best children's ministry volunteers I've met over the years aren't the most talented—they're the most loving. Kids can smell fake a mile away. But when they sense you truly care, they'll listen. They'll open up. They'll grow.

This is why burnout in ministry is such a danger—not just to us, but to the kids we lead. When love runs dry, we become like Spurgeon's example of a blacksmith with no fire, or a builder without mortar. We might still go through the motions, but we've lost our impact. That's why it's so critical to protect our hearts from bitterness, distraction, and weariness. Ask yourself regularly, "Do I still love this?" And more importantly, "Do I still love them?" If the answer is no, be honest about it. Pull back, rest, and reconnect with Jesus. He's the Shepherd. He'll restore your soul.

Another major takeaway from this chapter is the work itself. Feeding lambs is not glamorous. It's often unseen, underappreciated, and exhausting. Spurgeon says no one knows a shepherd's name. That may be truer today than ever. There's no spotlight in changing diapers in the nursery. No headlines for reading a Bible story to three squirrely second graders. No trophies for leading a small group of fifth grade boys through the life of David. But make no mistake—God sees it all. Every lesson prepared, every prayer whispered, every moment spent with a child pointing them to Jesus—it matters.

And here's the thing: lambs can't eat just anything. They need truth. We're not entertainers—we're spiritual feeders. In an age where entertainment is king, it's tempting to think your kids' ministry needs to be louder, flashier, and funnier to keep their attention. But fun doesn't feed the soul. It might grab attention, but it won't grow faith. Our kids need doctrine. Not dry facts—but the living, breathing truth of God's Word. Tell them about sin. Tell them about the cross. Tell them about grace and forgiveness and heaven and hell. Don't dumb it down—explain it clearly. Give them the meat of the gospel. If we don't, the world is more than happy to fill in the blanks.

4. Feed Each Child According To Their Need

Feeding lambs is also careful, individual work. One size doesn't fit all. You don't feed a toddler the same way you feed a teenager. Likewise, we must be students of our students—listening, observing, and asking God for wisdom to know what each child needs. What one child needs is encouragement; another needs conviction. One needs the simple story of Zacchaeus; another may be ready for the deeper truths of Romans. Let's ask God to help us feed each lamb, not just dump out a one-size-fits-all bucket of grain.

This also means we must make space at the table for children impacted by disability or special needs. It's not optional. It's not an "extra" ministry for churches with more resources or staff. It is a biblical mandate. Jesus said, "Let the little children come to Me and do not hinder them." That includes every child—verbal or non-verbal, neurotypical or neurodivergent, ambulatory or in a wheelchair. A truly biblical church must reflect the heart of God, and God's heart has always bent toward the vulnerable, the marginalized, and the overlooked.

Ministering to families impacted by special needs isn't just about accessibility—it's about belonging. These families are often worn out, isolated, and unsure if there's a place for them in the church. Let's show them, without question, that there is. That we see them. That we honor their journey. That their children are not problems to be solved but image-bearers to be loved and discipled.

To feed each lamb according to their need means creating environments that are flexible, inclusive, and built with intentionality. It might mean sensory rooms, visual schedules, trained buddies, or simply a volunteer who knows how to make eye contact and listen patiently. It means equipping our teams to understand and engage kids who learn or communicate differently—not with fear or frustration, but with compassion and confidence.

Let's be leaders who do the careful, intentional work of feeding each lamb—just like the Good Shepherd does.

5. Feeding Must Be Ongoing

And finally—this is continuous work. You don't just feed a child once. You feed them again and again, day after day, week after week. Parents, don't underestimate the power of consistency. Those bedtime prayers, dinner table devotions, the way you model Christ at home— those are the meals that nourish the soul. Ministry leaders, don't give up if a child seems distracted or disinterested. You're planting seeds. You're laying a foundation. Keep going.

I'll close with this: there is a Lamb on the throne who understands our weariness. Jesus is not asking us to do anything He hasn't done Himself. He gave His life for the sheep. He still loves the lambs—your lambs—and He calls you to join Him in the work. So stay faithful. Stay humble. Stay fed. And above all, stay in love—with Jesus and with the ones He's entrusted to you.

Let's feed His lambs well.

~ 5 ~

OF SUCH IS THE KINGDOM OF HEAVEN

Jesus tells His disciples that the gospel brings a kingdom. But what kind of kingdom has no children in it? How could it grow without them? Jesus tells us that children are welcomed into this kingdom—not just a few here and there, but that "of such is the kingdom of God." I don't think we should move away from the plain meaning of those words or assume He only meant people like children. It's clear He meant actual children—the little ones who were right there with Him—when He said, "of such is the kingdom of God." Every kingdom has children in it, and so does Christ's kingdom. I'm inclined to agree with John Newton when he said that the majority of those currently in heaven are children. When I think about the countless babies and young children who have died and are now in heaven, it's an amazing thought. While generation after generation of adults have passed away in unbelief and rebellion, countless multitudes of children have entered heaven—saved by God's grace through the death of Christ—and now sing His praises forever before His throne. "Of such is the kingdom of heaven." They set the tone and character of heaven—it's more of a kingdom of children than of adults.

Jesus tells us that the way to enter the kingdom is by receiving it: "Whoever does not receive the kingdom of God like a little child will never enter it." We don't enter the kingdom by solving a deep mystery or working something up within ourselves. We enter the kingdom by receiving something into ourselves. The kingdom comes into us, and we come into it—by receiving it. If entering God's kingdom required intense study or deep thinking, very few children could make it. But it's something to be received, which means even a child can do it. Those children old enough to sin and believe can hear the gospel and accept it by faith—and they do, with the help of the Holy Spirit. There's no question about that, because we've seen so many do it. I won't try to say exactly what age a child can first know Christ, but I will say it's much earlier than some people think. We've seen children who gave clear evidence of saving faith at a young age. Some died full of hope in Christ; others lived faithful lives, and some of them are now adults, active and honorable members of the church.

We also know that infants enter the kingdom. We're convinced that every infant who dies is included in God's chosen people and shares in the redemption Jesus won. No matter what others may believe, everything about God's Word and His nature leads us to believe that babies who die are saved. But how do they receive the kingdom? After all, Jesus said we must receive it the same way they do. Babies don't receive the kingdom by being born into the right family. John's gospel clearly tells us that being children of God doesn't come through family bloodlines or human will. Ancestry no longer gives anyone spiritual privilege. A baby won't enter heaven just because their parents were believers, and no child will be excluded because their parents were unbelievers. I firmly believe that a child of a Muslim, Catholic, Buddhist, or even a cannibal, who dies in infancy, is just as surely saved as a child of a Christian. There's no salvation by family or culture—infants are saved purely by God's will and grace. He made them His own.

A child who dies in China or Japan is just as saved as one who dies in England or America. Dark-skinned babies from African villages and little ones from Native American homes are just as welcomed. That proves they aren't saved by some external ritual or by the power of a priest. They are brought into God's kingdom by His free and sovereign grace. How are they saved, then? By good works? No—they've never done any. By innocence? No—if their innocence could have saved them, it should also have kept them from suffering or dying. But they do suffer and die. That shows they are affected by sin somehow. The sin that causes them to die proves they share in the fallen nature of Adam. They suffer the sad consequences of being born into a fallen world. We see their pleading eyes as they suffer, as if they're asking why they have to go through such pain. We grieve, knowing we can't fix it, and we're reminded of how deeply our entire human race is connected in Adam's fall. The pain of a dying child is one of the clearest proofs that we all share in the results of sin.

But thank God, those little ones live again—because Jesus died and rose again. They die physically because of a sin they didn't commit, but they live eternally through a righteousness they didn't earn—the righteousness of Jesus Christ, who redeemed them. We don't know all the details, but we believe they are spiritually reborn before entering heaven, because "what is born of the flesh is flesh," and to enter a spiritual kingdom, one must be born of the Spirit. However it happens, it's clear they aren't saved by intellect, choice, or actions, but by grace alone—nothing they did or felt played a part. And that's exactly how you must enter the kingdom—entirely by God's grace, not because of any goodness or strength of your own. You'll be saved by grace just as much as if you had never lived a righteous life or done a single good thing.

Now let's think about another group of children—those who grow past infancy and are old enough to knowingly sin, hear the gospel, and be saved. Many of these children do enter the kingdom by faith. And the way they receive the kingdom is the way we must receive it. So how do children receive the gospel? With humility, with simple trust, and without the distractions of worldly thinking. Of course, children aren't perfect examples in every way—they have their faults—but in this area, they show us how it's done. When a child hears the gospel, if God blesses that message, the child receives it without wrestling with doubts or mental roadblocks. A man might come to hear the gospel thinking Jesus was just a man—his prejudice gets in the way. Another person might come with all sorts of skepticism or false teachings he's picked up over the years—these block his ability to accept the truth. Another is full of self-righteousness or dependent on rituals or religion. These ideas clutter his heart and keep him from receiving Christ.

But a child? A child listens and receives. They don't carry those heavy ideas. They don't even know such obstacles exist. That innocence is a blessing. The child simply takes in the story of Jesus with a soft heart and prays:

> *Gentle Jesus, meek and mild,*
> *Look on me, a little child!*
> *Pity my simplicity;*
> *Let me come and rest in Thee.*

This freedom from preconceived notions is something we all desperately need. Just like your son or daughter must come in simple faith, so must you. Whether you're a pastor or a scholar, a philosopher or a farmer—there's only one way in. Children receive Christ humbly. They don't think they can earn it or deserve it. In all my life, I don't think I've ever met a child who had to overcome self-righteousness to come to Jesus.

Reflections from Ryan

Today's Kingdom Kids

Charles Spurgeon's reminder that "of such is the kingdom of heaven" carries massive implications for those of us called to lead, serve, or parent the next generation. These aren't just poetic words from the past—they're marching orders for today's children's ministry leaders, parents, and spiritual mentors. We live in a world that is increasingly distracted, anxious, and skeptical. But Jesus' words still cut through the noise: children matter deeply to God. And not only that—they belong in His kingdom.

Let that sink in. Jesus didn't say, "Let them visit." He said the kingdom is made up of them. That changes everything.

If you're leading kids at church or raising them at home, this truth should light a fire in your heart. We're not just babysitting. We're not filling time with games and crafts. We're discipling citizens of God's kingdom.

1. Kids Aren't Just Welcome—They're Essential

One of the enemy's greatest lies is that children are somehow "less than" when it comes to spiritual things. That they're too young to understand the gospel. That they'll "get it later." But Spurgeon, echoing Jesus, reminds us that the kingdom belongs to them—right now. Not when they turn 18. Not when they graduate high school. Now.

We must adjust our ministries and parenting accordingly. We should expect big things from little hearts. We should teach deep truths in age-appropriate ways. We should look for signs of spiritual hunger and growth, and then water those seeds with love, truth, and grace.

I've seen a child with special needs pray with more sincerity than many adults. I've watched 2nd graders weep over their friends who don't know Jesus. The Holy Spirit doesn't use a "junior" version of Himself in children. He speaks, calls, convicts, and comforts—right there on the floor of the preschool room or in the back seat of the car.

Let's believe, like Spurgeon did, that the majority in heaven may very well be children. Let's take seriously our call to shepherd the flock that Jesus Himself says is the model of kingdom citizenship.

2. We Must Remove Barriers—Not Build Them

Jesus said we must receive the kingdom like a little child—with humility and faith. But often, we unintentionally make the gospel harder than it needs to be for kids. We attach expectations, rules, or complicated theology before helping them fall in love with Jesus.

Spurgeon points out that adults come with intellectual pride, bad theology, or worldly distractions. But kids? They come open. Curious. Eager to believe.

That means our job isn't to overcomplicate. It's to clarify. To simplify without watering down. To strip away the clutter of religion and point them to the cross.

A humble heart is more important than a sharp mind. And a child's natural openness is a beautiful thing that we should protect, not rush through. In our ministry spaces, let's make room for questions. Let's tell the old, old story in ways that capture their imaginations. Let's help them understand that receiving the gospel doesn't require jumping through hoops—it requires an open heart.

3. Salvation Is by Grace Alone—For All Ages

Spurgeon makes a powerful point: babies who die are not saved by innocence or family heritage—they're saved by God's sovereign grace. And that same grace is what every child (and adult) needs.

This humbles us. It also gives us hope.

We don't need to be perfect parents or flawless leaders. Our work is important, but it is God who saves. Our role is to plant and water. God gives the growth.

This is freeing for the large group leader who feels like the lesson didn't "land." It's freeing for the parent who worries their child isn't "getting it." Keep pointing them to Jesus. Keep praying. Keep showing up. Grace does what we cannot.

4. Kids Are Capable of Real Faith

One of the most exciting and encouraging truths in this chapter is that children are capable of real, authentic, saving faith. Spurgeon wasn't interested in sentimental spirituality. He believed that children could repent, believe, and live as disciples of Jesus. And so should we.

But to see that happen, we need to give them the chance.

Do you give kids in your ministry space opportunities to respond to Jesus?

Do you encourage faith conversations at home?

Are you listening for signs of spiritual awakening in your children or your students?

Let's not assume they'll "get serious" later. Let's lean into what God is already doing in them now.

I know kids who've led their parents to Christ. I know elementary-age students who pray over their sick classmates with boldness and faith. I know preteens who serve faithfully in their churches and stand up for Jesus at school.

Don't underestimate what a child can do with the Holy Spirit living inside them.

5. We Enter the Kingdom the Same Way

Here's the final twist: Spurgeon's not just talking about children. He's talking about us.

Jesus says we must become like children to enter the kingdom. We have to let go of our pride, our assumptions, our baggage, and simply receive. That should challenge us.

Are we modeling the kind of faith we want to see in our kids? Are we open, humble, and teachable? Or are we caught up in trying to impress God with our "grown-up" spirituality?

Children show us the way—not because they're perfect, but because they're dependent. They know they need help. They know how to trust. They aren't afraid to ask questions. They don't overthink grace—they just receive it.

Let's learn from them.

Final Thoughts

If you're in children's ministry, keep showing up. Keep planting seeds. Keep telling the story of Jesus with joy and passion. The kingdom belongs to the kids you're ministering to—and your work is not in vain.

If you're a parent, take heart. You don't have to have all the answers. You just have to keep pointing your kids to the One who does. Read the Bible together. Pray together. Worship together. Let your home be a mini-church where faith is nurtured.

Jesus values children. Jesus receives children. And Jesus calls us to do the same.

Let's never forget: the kingdom of heaven doesn't tolerate children—it belongs to them.

~ 6 ~

AS A LITTLE CHILD

When our Lord blessed the little children, He was on His final journey to Jerusalem. This blessing was part of His farewell, and it reminds us that some of His last words to His disciples before ascending to heaven were the tender command: "Feed My lambs." That deep concern for children was strong in the heart of the Good Shepherd of Israel, "who gathers the lambs in His arms and carries them close to His heart." It makes perfect sense that on His farewell journey, He would stop to pour out His loving blessing on the children.

Today, Jesus isn't physically with us, but we know exactly where He is—enthroned in heaven, with all power in heaven and on earth to bless His people. So let's draw near to Him. Let's seek His presence through fellowship and lean on His prayers on our behalf. Let's pray not only for ourselves but also for others—and let's give children, especially our own and others, a top priority in those prayers. We know more about Jesus now than the women of Palestine did. Shouldn't we be even more eager than they were to bring our children to Him, so He can bless them and welcome them just like He has welcomed us? Jesus still delights in blessing. He hasn't changed, and His grace hasn't run out. Just as He continues to welcome sinners, He still blesses children. Whether you're a parent or a teacher, don't be satisfied until you know He's received your children and blessed them in a way that shows they belong to the kingdom of God.

When Jesus saw that His disciples were not only hesitant to let the children come to Him but even scolded those who brought them, He was deeply upset. He called the children to Himself to correct their thinking. He told them clearly that children were not intruders—they were very welcome. In fact, children and those with childlike hearts are exactly the kind of people His kingdom is made up of. More than that, He declared that no one can enter that kingdom unless they come in the same way a child does. He spoke with divine authority, starting with His serious phrase "Truly, I tell you," and backed it up with the power of His own words, "I say to you." These strong statements demand our full attention. Children aren't just allowed in the kingdom—they show us the very way to enter it.

It's clear the disciples thought children were too unimportant to be worth Jesus' time. If it had been a royal figure wanting to see Jesus, Peter and the others would have rolled out the red carpet. But these were just poor moms with babies, boys, and girls. If an adult like themselves had come, they wouldn't have turned him away. But mere kids? Nursing babies and toddlers? Surely Jesus had more important things to do! The disciples figured these little ones weren't worth bothering Him. But if we're talking about being insignificant, who among us deserves God's attention? If children are too small to matter to Jesus, then what about us? He calls whole islands "a very small thing," sees humanity as grasshoppers, and says we are like nothing at all. If we're humble, we'd ask, "Lord, what is man that You are mindful of him?" If God cares about sparrows, and not one falls without His knowledge, don't you think He cares even more for children? Let's get rid of the idea that anyone is too small for God's love. "Though the Lord is exalted, He cares for the lowly." And are children really so insignificant? Don't they make up a huge part of heaven's population? Isn't it your belief—and mine—that many who walk heaven's streets are children? Taken from this life before they sinned, they skipped the hardships of this world and now constantly look into the face of our heavenly Father. "The kingdom of God belongs to such as these." Still think they're unimportant? These children, who make up such a large portion of God's elect? Dare we overlook them? In fact, we could say it's adults who are few in number among the saved. And many children do grow up—so we should never think a child is insignificant. A child becomes a man. In him lie potential and purpose. Though his adulthood isn't visible yet, it's there—and to harm it is to harm the future man. If you mess with the heart of a boy, you might destroy the soul of a man. A small lie in a child's ear can become deadly poison in a man's heart. Bad seeds sown in childhood grow into weeds that may choke a man's life. But if truth is planted in a young heart, it can flourish, bearing fruit in adulthood. That child listening to a soft-spoken teacher may one day grow into a Martin Luther who shakes the world with truth. Who knows? A boy with truth in his heart may grow up to fear the Lord and help keep the faith alive in this dark world. So don't overlook the young or think they don't matter. They deserve a front-row seat. If someone must be pushed to the back, let it not be the children. The past is gone, and even the present is slipping away—but the future belongs to our kids. So make way for the children. Make space for the boys and girls!

Maybe the disciples also thought children were too silly or playful. They'd see Jesus as just part of a game—getting hugged by Him might be fun, but they wouldn't grasp how serious it was. Trivial, they'd say. But who are the real triflers—children or adults? Isn't it adults who waste their lives chasing pleasure or spending all their time dressing up for show? And what about those who hoard wealth just to have it? That's adult-level triviality—child's play without the joy. Kids play with toys—they're supposed to. But I've seen adults play with their souls, with heaven and hell, with God's Word, and even with God Himself. So don't accuse kids of being shallow. Their games are often more meaningful than adult pursuits. Half the time, political debates and wars are less noble than a child's play. If the world's full of foolishness, don't be surprised to find it in grown-ups even more than in kids.

Some might say, "Even if Jesus blesses the children, they'll forget it." His loving look, His holy words—it'll all fade once they're back to their games. But let's be real—don't adults forget too? Don't most preachers constantly repeat themselves to congregations who forget everything by Monday? The Bible describes people who hear truth, look in a mirror, and walk away forgetting what they saw. Don't accuse children of forgetfulness—it might reflect more on us than them.

And do kids really forget? Isn't it true that the memories we hold onto in old age are usually from early childhood? I've shaken hands with elderly men who remember hymns sung at their mother's side, but can't recall last week. Childhood memories stick. The blessing from Jesus would've burned itself into those young hearts forever. His smile, His words—they would not be forgotten. Sorry, Peter, James, and John—Jesus knew better. Let the children come to Him.

Maybe the disciples thought children just couldn't understand. Jesus' teachings were deep—how could kids grasp them? But that's a mistake. Children connect easily with Jesus' words. They learn to read faster from the New Testament than any other book. His words are simple and made for them. Kids understand the child Jesus better than anyone. What kind of understanding do they need? Faith? Children are better at faith than adults. They haven't yet been jaded by lies, broken trust, or cynicism. Let the Holy Spirit guide that natural faith, and it will bear fruit.

Do children lack the ability to repent? Absolutely not. Haven't we seen a little girl cry herself sick from guilt? Or a boy with a conscience so tender that he's miserable after doing wrong? I remember my own childhood conviction—my longing for forgiveness began young. God's Spirit can work repentance in children; that's not a theory, that's a fact many of us have lived.

What else do kids lack—understanding? Of what? If Jesus' message were modern, complex philosophy, maybe they'd be left out. But the gospel is the poor man's Bible. Its truths are simple. Sure, there are deep mysteries, but salvation doesn't require diving to the bottom of them. What's needed to be saved is so clear, a child can understand. Jesus crucified isn't some puzzle for scholars—it's truth for regular people. It's both meat for men and milk for babies.

Did someone say children can't love? That's one of the most beautiful parts of being a Christian. And no one can deny that kids are full of love. If only we adults loved like they do!

In short, the disciples thought the kids weren't ready because they weren't like them. Not tall enough. Not grown-up enough. Not serious enough. But Jesus flips the script: "Don't say the child must become like the man. You must become like the child." That's the real message. Adults must grow down. "Unless you receive the kingdom of God like a little child, you will never enter it." His words silence all objections. We shouldn't wish our children were more like us—maybe we should wish we were more like them. A fresh start, a clean slate, a childlike heart—these are what we need. "Unless someone is born again, he cannot see the kingdom of God." "Unless you change and become like little children, you will not enter the kingdom of heaven."

Now I wonder—do you still carry the disciples' attitude deep inside? It used to be common: old folks were skeptical of child conversions. They frowned at letting kids join the church. They'd say, "They're just a bunch of girls and boys," like that made them less. If a child died shortly after conversion, everyone believed it was real. But if the child lived, suddenly they were tested and doubted. They had to pass doctrinal quizzes and act like mini-adults. A young convert wasn't allowed to play or speak like a kid anymore. People expected him to instantly mature twenty years. But that's nowhere in Scripture. Unfortunately, people valued opinions and tradition more than the Word of God. They made kids wait years before being allowed inside the church family.

If that kind of thinking still lingers in your heart, get rid of it. It's just plain wrong. If a man and a child gave the same testimony of faith, I have no reason to believe the man over the child. In fact, if I had to be cautious, I'd lean more toward doubting the adult. Children are less likely to fake it and less likely to parrot religious phrases. So take it from the Lord Himself—don't try to make kids more like you. You be transformed until you are more like them.

Reflections from Ryan

Room for the Kids

Charles Spurgeon's chapter, As a Little Child, hits at something we must never lose sight of: the place of children in the heart of Jesus—and in the heart of the Church. His words are like a spotlight exposing the ways we unintentionally minimize children's faith. And while Spurgeon was writing in the 1800s, I can tell you as someone who's been in children's ministry for decades—these same attitudes still creep into our churches today.

Let's start here: Jesus made time for children. Not as an afterthought. Not as a feel-good photo op. But as a matter of Kingdom priority. The same Jesus who rebuked storms, raised the dead, and walked on water got "much displeased" when His disciples tried to block children from getting to Him. That says something.

If you're a KidMin leader or a parent, I want to challenge you with this: Are you making space for kids to encounter Jesus—or are you unintentionally blocking the way?

That might sound harsh. But sometimes we do this subtly. We assume kids aren't ready to understand deep spiritual truths. Or we think they're just playing and not paying attention. Or we figure they'll have their "real" faith moment when they're older—maybe in the youth group or as adults. That's not how Jesus saw it. And if that's not how He saw it, it can't be how we operate.

Let me remind you of a powerful truth: Children can and do experience real, lasting faith in Jesus. I've seen it. I've lived it. Some of the strongest testimonies of lifelong faith I've ever heard started in children's ministry. They began with a faithful Sunday school teacher, a moment at VBS, or a gentle word during prayer time. Spurgeon says, "They are the world's future." I would add: They're also the Church's present.

We must stop measuring a child's spiritual depth based on how many Bible verses they can recite. Or how still they sit during worship. Or how "adult-like" their faith looks. Jesus never once told a child to grow up before coming to Him. In fact, He told us that unless we become like them, we won't even enter His Kingdom. That's humbling.

You see, children have a faith that's uncluttered. They don't come with years of skepticism. They believe God is who He says He is. They take His promises at face value. That's not weakness—that's spiritual strength. It's the kind of faith we all need to return to.

As ministry leaders, our job is not to polish kids into little theologians but to guide their hearts toward Jesus. We plant seeds. We water. We pray. And sometimes, we get the joy of seeing God do something right in front of us.

So how do we put this into practice?

1. Raise Your Expectations for What God Can Do in a Child's Life

Kids are not "junior" Christians. If they have the Holy Spirit, they have full access to everything He offers. Don't lower the bar for them spiritually. Raise it—and give them the tools to meet it. Equip them to hear God's voice, memorize Scripture, and serve others.

2. Make Ministry With Kids, Not Just For Kids

We often build entire ministries for kids—but not with them. Get them involved. Let them serve. Let them lead in worship. Let them pray. Let them welcome new kids. They don't need to wait until they're 18 to be useful in the Kingdom.

3. Be a Champion, Not a Gatekeeper

Spurgeon reminds us that the disciples tried to be gatekeepers. Jesus wasn't impressed. Parents and leaders—let's be champions instead. Celebrate when kids take steps of faith. Believe them when they say they've trusted Jesus. Walk with them through the hard questions. Don't block the way—open the gate wider.

4. Teach Truths in Ways Kids Can Grasp

The gospel doesn't need to be dumbed down—it needs to be clearly explained. Jesus used stories, questions, and visuals. Do the same. Use object lessons. Use humor. Make it sticky. Help kids see how Scripture connects to their everyday lives. Remember: the gospel is simple enough for a child to understand, yet deep enough to challenge a scholar.

5. Stop Treating Childlike Faith as Less Than

Spurgeon's words cut deep: "It is the man who must grow down and become like a child." Somewhere along the way, many of us started thinking our theological degrees and adult responsibilities made us more spiritual than the 8-year-old praying in her room. But Jesus sees that 8-year-old. He treasures her faith. We should, too.

6. Recognize the Long-Term Impact of Early Spiritual Seeds

A conversation you have with a child today may not seem like much. But thirty years from now, that same child may be the one leading worship, planting a church, or raising the next generation of godly kids. Don't underestimate the power of one Spirit-led moment. Eternity is long—and God is always at work.

7. Celebrate Spiritual Milestones Early and Often

When a child places their faith in Jesus, don't hesitate. Celebrate it. Affirm it. Baptize them. Disciple them. Help them see that their faith matters now—not just later. Too many kids fall away in their teens not because they didn't believe—but because the Church didn't affirm or disciple them when they did.

Final Thoughts

Let me close with this: I believe the next revival will come through children. I really do. They are hungry. They are open. And they are ready—if we are ready to make room.

If we're going to reach the world, we must start with the kids. The disciples got it wrong that day when they tried to send the children away. But Jesus got it right—and still does. He made room for the little ones. Let's do the same.

So to every parent, teacher, and ministry leader reading this: keep planting seeds. Keep believing in the power of childlike faith. Keep making space at the feet of Jesus for the smallest among us. Because in the eyes of heaven, those small ones are often the greatest of all.

~ 7 ~

FEED MY LAMBS

The reason for feeding the lambs was to be for his Master's sake—not for himself. If Peter had been the first pope of Rome, and if he had been anything like those who followed him—which he certainly wasn't—then maybe the Lord would have said, "Feed your sheep. I'm putting them in your hands, Peter, Vicar of Christ on earth." But no, not at all. Peter was to feed them, but they weren't his—they still belonged to Christ. The work you do for Jesus, brothers and sisters, is not for your own benefit. Your Sunday School classes are not your kids—they are Christ's. Paul gave this instruction: "Feed the church of God," and Peter himself later wrote in his letter, "Shepherd God's flock that is among you, watching over them—not because you have to, but because you want to; not for selfish gain, but with a willing heart." No matter what these lambs grow up to be, the glory belongs to the Master, not the servant. Every moment spent, every bit of energy and effort poured out, is for the praise of the One who owns the lambs.

Yet while this is a selfless task, it's also a truly honorable one—and we can step into it knowing it's one of the most noble things we could ever do. Jesus said, "My lambs. My sheep." Think about that—and let it amaze you that Jesus would entrust them to us. Poor Peter! I imagine he felt pretty awkward when that breakfast began. If I were in his shoes, I'd have had a hard time even making eye contact with Jesus, remembering how I had denied Him with cursing and swearing. But our Lord wanted to put Peter at ease by getting him to talk about the love that had recently come into question. Like a skilled doctor, Jesus went right to the sore spot, asking, "Do you love Me?" It wasn't that Jesus didn't know Peter's heart—it was that Peter needed to be sure of it himself, to give a new, sincere confession: "Yes, Lord, You know I love You." Jesus was about to have a tender but necessary conversation with Peter, so there'd never again be anything between them. When Peter said, "Yes, Lord, You know I love You," you might have expected Jesus to reply, "I love you too, Peter"—but He didn't say that, and yet, He really did. Maybe Peter didn't catch it, but we can see it more clearly—our minds aren't as foggy as Peter's was that unforgettable morning. Jesus was saying, "I love you so much, I trust you with what I bought with My own blood. The most precious thing I have in the world—My flock—I'm entrusting to you. Simon, I believe in your love for Me so deeply, I'm making you a shepherd. These sheep are everything to Me—I gave My life for them. Now, Simon, son of John, take care of them for Me." Oh, what grace that was! That was the tender heart of Christ saying, "Dear Peter, come close and share in what I care about most." Jesus believed Peter's love so deeply that He didn't just say it—He showed it. Three times He repeated it: "Feed My lambs. Feed My sheep. Feed My sheep." That's how much He loved Peter. When Jesus deeply loves someone, He gives them something important to do—or something hard to go through.

Many of us were rescued like sticks pulled from a fire. We were once "God's enemies through our evil actions"—and now we're part of His church and counted among His friends. And He trusts us with His most precious ones. I sometimes wonder—when the prodigal son returned home and the father welcomed him back—did the father send him to the market on market day, trusting him to sell the wheat and bring back the money? Most people would probably say, "I'm glad he's home—but I'll still send the older brother to do the business, since he's always been faithful." Yet in my case, Jesus welcomed me like a prodigal, and it wasn't long before He trusted me with the gospel—the greatest treasure of all. What a sign of love that was! I can't think of anything greater. The mission given to Peter shows how completely Jesus had forgiven him—He restored the very one who had denied Him and told him to care for His lambs and sheep. Oh, what a beautiful task! Not for yourself, yet somehow it is. The one who serves only himself loses everything, but the one who loses himself in service actually finds the greatest reward of all.

The main motivation for a good shepherd is love. We are to feed Christ's lambs because we love Him.

First, it's a proof of love. "If you love Me, keep My commandments." If you love Me, feed My lambs. If you love Christ, show it—show it by doing good to others, by pouring yourself out to help them, so Jesus can rejoice over their growth.

Second, it's the overflow of love. Feed My lambs. Even if your love for Christ is small when you start helping others, it will grow quickly. Love gets stronger when you use it. It's like a blacksmith's arm—wielding the hammer builds its strength. Love loves until it loves more, and then more, and more still—until it loves to the fullest, and even then it isn't satisfied. It keeps reaching to better reflect the perfect love of Christ Jesus, our Savior.

And beyond being the overflow of love, feeding the lambs is the expression of love. Haven't we told the Lord we loved Him in the middle of teaching or preaching? I'm sure many teachers feel their love for Jesus more vividly while they're with their class than when they're home alone. Someone might sit at home and groan out:

> 'Tis a point I long to know,
> Often it brings anxious thought,

and they'll wipe their forehead, rub their eyes, and fall deeper into gloom. But if they'd get up and do something for Jesus, that question they're wrestling with would get answered quickly. Love would start pouring out of their heart until there'd be no more doubt it was there.

So let's stay in this joyful service to Jesus. Let it be the delight of love—the ocean it swims in, the sunlight it soaks in. For a heart full of love, the greatest joy is working for Christ. And one of the most rewarding and joyful ways to do that is helping young believers grow in understanding, so they can become strong in the Lord.

Reflections from Ryan

A Revolutionary Concept

Jesus didn't say, "Run great events for My lambs" or "Keep them entertained for Me." He said, "Feed My lambs." That phrase has stuck with me for years—and the more I think about it, the more I realize how revolutionary it is for children's ministry leaders and parents alike.

Feeding lambs is personal. It's tender. It's intentional. It's not about performance, programming, or polished presentations. It's about spiritual nourishment—giving kids what they need to grow strong in the Lord.

1. These Lambs Aren't Yours—They're His

Spurgeon hit the nail on the head here: your ministry kids, your Sunday morning class, your own children at home—they ultimately belong to Jesus, not to you. You're not raising or leading them for your own glory. You're caring for kids that He purchased with His own blood. That perspective changes everything.

When we treat ministry like it's ours, we start focusing on results, numbers, applause, or even reputation. But when we realize these are His lambs, we approach everything with a deeper sense of humility and reverence.

That means the hard days matter just as much as the highlight reels. When you're holding a crying toddler in the nursery or dealing with a fifth grader who just won't listen, remember—Jesus sees that moment. It matters to Him. Those lambs are His.

2. Ministry Is Both Humbling And Honoring

It's humbling because, like Peter, we've all blown it. We've had our moments of fear, denial, distraction, and discouragement. And yet—Jesus still says to each of us, "Feed My lambs." He invites us into His mission not because we're perfect, but because we love Him.

That's what struck me about Spurgeon's words: Jesus didn't just restore Peter. He reinstated him to leadership and entrusted him with what mattered most. That's grace in action.

But this work is also honoring. What an incredible thing—that the King of kings would trust you with His flock. The fact that you get to open up the Bible to a group of 7-year-olds, or tuck in your 3-year-old at night with a prayer, is sacred. Don't let the routine of ministry make you forget that.

3. Love Is The Motivation For It All

"If you love Me, feed My lambs." Jesus didn't say, "If you have a degree," or "If you feel confident," or "If you have an Instagram-worthy environment." He simply asked Peter, "Do you love Me?"

Love is what makes ordinary ministry extraordinary. If you're waiting to feel qualified or ready, you might be waiting forever. But if you love Jesus—you're ready right now. That love is the reason we show up, the reason we lead with grace, and the reason we keep going when we're exhausted.

And the more you serve, the more that love grows. Like Spurgeon said, love gets stronger the more you use it. I've seen that in my own life. There have been seasons when I've felt spiritually dry or distracted—but when I step in to teach a lesson, or sit with a hurting kid, or pray with a volunteer—I feel that love for Jesus come alive again. Ministry fuels relationship.

4. Serving Kids Is A Spiritual Workout

I like how Spurgeon compared love to a blacksmith's arm. Strength doesn't come from sitting still—it comes from consistent effort. When you're in the trenches of kids' ministry or parenting, don't forget: this is how spiritual muscles are built.

That Sunday morning when nothing goes right? That Wednesday night when no one seems to be listening? That car ride when your child asks a big spiritual question you weren't ready for? Those are workouts. They're forming your character and your calling.

It's also why we can't feed lambs on an empty stomach. If you're going to help children grow in faith, you need to be growing too. Don't just pour out—make sure you're being poured into. Stay connected to the Word. Stay connected to community. Stay connected to Jesus.

5. The Simple Things Matter Most

Spurgeon pointed out how love flows naturally when we serve. That's true—but let me take it a step further. Love grows in the small, unseen, and often overlooked moments of ministry and parenting.

Reading one Bible verse with your child before school. Sending a postcard to a first-time visitor. Praying over a kid's name card before they arrive. Smiling at the parent who feels overwhelmed. These things may not feel like much—but they are food for the soul.

Don't underestimate the power of presence. You don't have to have all the answers. You just have to show up consistently with the heart of Jesus.

6. Feed The Lambs, Don't Just Entertain Them

There's a lot of pressure today to make children's ministry fun, loud, and fast-paced—and yes, joy and energy are important! But if we're not feeding kids the Word of God and helping them know Jesus, we're missing the point.

Fun should be the wrapping paper, not the gift.

Your job is not just to keep kids busy—it's to build spiritual foundations. That means teaching Bible truth clearly. It means modeling godly character. It means creating environments where kids feel safe, seen, and spiritually stretched.

And if you're a parent, the same applies. Your home is the primary place for discipleship. Don't leave it all to the church. Read with your kids. Pray with them. Talk about Jesus in everyday moments.

7. Jesus Trusts You—And He's With You

One of the most powerful parts of this chapter is the fact that Jesus looked Peter in the eye—after all his failures—and said, "I still trust you." That should bring tears to our eyes. We don't earn this. We don't deserve this. But we are called, commissioned, and empowered by grace.

Jesus could've chosen angels to teach kids—but He chose you. And He doesn't just send you—He goes with you.

So when you feel like giving up, remember this: You're not alone in the work. The Chief Shepherd sees every seed you plant, every lamb you feed, every hour you invest. And He will be faithful to bring fruit in His time.

Final Thoughts

So friend—whether you're leading a preschool classroom, raising toddlers, pastoring a kids' ministry, or volunteering once a month—lean into the words of Jesus: "Feed My lambs."

It's a holy calling. It's a worthy mission. And it's the kind of work that echoes in eternity.

~ 8 ~

THE CHILD TIMOTHY
AND HIS TEACHERS

Today, since there are sadly so few Christian mothers and grandmothers in the world, the church has wisely stepped in to supplement what kids may miss at home by providing teaching under her loving care. Children without Christian parents are taken under the church's wing. I believe this is a truly wonderful and godly practice. I'm thankful for all the brothers and sisters who dedicate their Sundays—and often many of their weekday evenings—to teaching other people's children, who soon begin to feel like their own. They take on the role of spiritual fathers and mothers, serving these children for God's sake, and they are doing something very right.

Let no Christian parent believe the lie that Sunday school was created to take over their responsibility. The original and most natural design is for Christian parents to raise their children in the instruction and care of the Lord. Godly grandparents and faithful moms and dads must make sure their kids are well taught from the Bible. Where Christian parents are missing, it's good and right for godly men and women to step in. It is Christlike to take on a role that others have neglected. Jesus takes joy in those who feed His lambs and care for His little ones—He doesn't want even one of them to be lost. Timothy had the great blessing of being taught by his family—those who were responsible for him. But when that blessing isn't available, we must do our best to fill the gap and help children overcome the loss. So step up, passionate men and women—set yourselves apart for this joyful work.

Now take note of what Timothy was taught. "From childhood you have known the Holy Scriptures"—he was taught to deeply respect the Word of God. That phrase "Holy Scriptures" is worth emphasizing. One of the first goals of any Sunday school should be to help kids honor the Bible and understand that these writings are sacred and inspired. The Jewish people valued the Old Testament above all else. And though some became superstitious and missed the deeper meaning, they still deserve credit for their deep respect for God's Word. Today, we desperately need that same reverence.

I've met people with strange beliefs, and I'm not overly concerned by how odd their ideas are—but what truly alarms me is when they no longer care what Scripture says. If I prove their belief is unbiblical, they don't seem to mind—because they've stopped caring about the Bible altogether. That attitude is more dangerous than simply being mistaken. Disregard for Scripture is the great curse of the church today. We can tolerate differences of opinion if there's a sincere desire to follow God's Word. But if the Bible no longer holds any authority for you, then we're not on the same team—we're in different camps, and it's best to be honest about that. If we want to have a church that truly belongs to God, we must treat the Bible as holy and worthy of reverence. It's not made up of myths or passed down by luck. It is a divinely inspired revelation from our Holy God. We must teach our kids to love and respect it above all else. Tell them that the Bible is like silver refined seven times in a furnace—completely pure. Let their appreciation for God's Word reach the highest level.

Notice also that Timothy was taught not just to respect spiritual things in general, but to know the Scriptures. His mother and grandmother taught him the Bible. Now imagine we gather children on Sundays, but we just entertain them or fill the time with generic moral lessons—what have we really accomplished? Nothing worthy of the day or the church. Suppose we focus on teaching kids the rules of our denomination, but never open the Bible—what good is that? Our denominational guide might be right—or it might be wrong. But when we teach straight from the Bible, we can be confident we're teaching truth. The Bible is God's Word. When we teach it, we're teaching what God Himself will bless. Oh dear teachers—and I say this to myself too—let's make sure our teaching stays deeply rooted in Scripture! Don't stress if kids forget our own words; pray that they remember what God says. May truths about sin, righteousness, and judgment be written on their hearts! May the truths of God's love, Christ's grace, and the Spirit's power never fade from their memory! May they understand the necessity of Jesus' sacrifice, the power of His resurrection, and the hope of His return! Let the doctrines of grace be etched deep in their hearts, never to be erased. If we can accomplish that, our lives won't be wasted. This generation may be drifting away from God's truth—but if we instill the gospel into the hearts of the next, we still have hope.

There's one more thing: young Timothy's childhood training was effective. Paul says, "You have known the Holy Scriptures." That's a big statement. You might say, "I've taught children the Bible," but whether they know it is another matter. And let me ask: do you know the Scriptures? Even with all the knowledge available today, biblical knowledge is rare. If we held a Bible quiz right now, some of you might not score very well. But Timothy, even as a young boy, knew the Scriptures—he had a strong understanding. That's not out of reach for today's kids. With God's help, your children can understand all that's necessary to be saved. They can understand sin like their parents do, grasp the meaning of the cross like their grandparents, and trust in Jesus just like any adult. The gospel is not complicated—it's simple enough for a child to grasp. In fact, grown-ups must become like children to enter the kingdom. So lay a solid foundation. Don't rush or do Sunday school carelessly. Help the children truly know the Bible. Let Scripture—not any man-made book—be your go-to guide.

This kind of training needs to be powered by saving faith. The Bible doesn't save on its own, but it can make someone wise enough to be saved. A child might know the Bible and still not be born again. Salvation comes through believing in Jesus. Many kids are called by God so early they don't remember the exact moment it happened—but they were truly saved. You might not be able to say exactly when the sun rose this morning, but it still did. The same is true of salvation. Whether we see the moment or not, it happens when a child truly believes in Jesus. Maybe Timothy's mother and grandmother taught him the Old Testament before they even knew Christ themselves. If so, they gave him the pieces of the puzzle without the picture—but even that was valuable, because it was all they knew. How much greater our privilege is now, since we can clearly teach about Jesus using the New Testament to explain the Old! Can't we hope that our children might believe in Jesus even earlier than Timothy did? Even if a child doesn't know every doctrine, as soon as they trust in Jesus, they're saved. Faith in the Jesus revealed in Scripture will save anyone. "If you believe with all your heart, you may," said Philip to the Ethiopian man—and we say the same to every child. If you believe that Jesus is the Savior and you put your trust in Him, you are truly saved—just as much as someone with gray hair and decades of experience.

And it's through this faith in Jesus that we grow in our salvation. The moment we believe, we are saved—but we don't instantly become spiritually mature. That takes time. Faith starts small, but it helps us grow. Just like learning the alphabet—you start with A, B, and C by faith, and you continue to D, E, and F the same way—until one day you're fluent in the Book of God's wisdom. Start with simple faith, and that same faith will help you reach the deeper things. Sadly, many today chase "progress" through speculation and wild ideas. But faith—not doubt—is the true path forward. Doubt isn't a stepping-stone to truth; it's a trap. The real stepping-stones to eternal life are the promises of God, trusted by faith. So let's pray that our children will keep growing in knowledge and faith. Scripture can make them wise for salvation—but only through faith in Jesus Christ. That faith is our goal: faith in the chosen, risen, exalted Savior. That's the anchor we long for every child to have—because it will hold them steady for life.

When solid teaching of Scripture is combined with genuine faith, it produces strong, stable character. A person who has known the Bible since childhood and puts their faith in Jesus will be grounded in the unchanging truth of God's Word.

Oh, teachers—do you see the difference you can make? In your classrooms sit future evangelists. That child in the toddler room might grow up to be a missionary. The young girl in your class may one day become a spiritual mother in the church. That energetic boy might carry God's banner into spiritual battle. Every time your class meets, you're shaping the future. May God help you do it well! And we pray together, with one heart, that the Lord Jesus will bless our Sunday schools now and until He comes again.

reflections from Ryan

The Timothy Challenge

If you're a parent, grandparent, pastor, or ministry volunteer, let me say this plainly: you matter more than you realize. You're in a long line of spiritual mentors that traces all the way back to people like Lois and Eunice—Timothy's grandmother and mother—whose faithful teaching helped launch one of the New Testament's most influential church leaders.

Spurgeon's message in this chapter is loud and clear: don't underestimate the power of early spiritual training. And I couldn't agree more. In fact, in today's fast-paced, distracted world, that kind of intentional spiritual investment is not only important—it's urgent.

Let's look at how we can live this out today.

1. The Church Is A Safety Net, Not A Substitute

Spurgeon starts with an important warning: The church is never meant to replace the home. That hits home for me. I've seen too many parents, even well-meaning ones, treat church like a spiritual daycare—drop the kids off, hope they learn something, and check the box for the week. But discipleship is a daily journey, not a weekly pit stop.

Now don't get me wrong—thank God for children's ministry teams! I've spent my life equipping and encouraging these heroes. But the best-case scenario is when church and home partner together. Parents plant the seeds all week long, and the church comes alongside to water and nurture them. If you're a parent reading this, don't outsource your influence. If you're a church leader, don't just teach kids—equip their families too.

2. Teaching Scripture Is The Non-Negotiable

I love that Spurgeon focuses on what Timothy was taught: the Holy Scriptures. Not just "nice stories" or "virtues and values"—but the very Word of God. That's what Lois and Eunice gave him. And that's what we need to give the next generation.

Let me get real with you. We've all seen it—ministries slowly shift from gospel-centered teaching to just "making it fun" or "teaching values." And yes, fun is important. Energy, creativity, engagement—they all matter. But fun is the vehicle, not the destination. If we're not faithfully teaching Scripture, we're missing the mark.

The Bible is living and active. It's not just information—it's transformation. So make sure your lessons, your conversations, and your parenting all point back to the truth of God's Word. The world is loud, but Scripture still speaks. Let's make sure kids are hearing it.

3. Love For The Bible Must Be Modeled

Spurgeon had strong words for people who no longer care about what the Bible says. And that same warning rings true today. Our culture is drowning in opinions, deconstruction, and confusion. Many have lost respect for the authority of God's Word.

But here's the good news: kids are watching us. They take their cues from how we respond to the Bible. If they see you opening it with excitement, praying its promises, and treating it like the treasure it is, that speaks volumes. If you're a parent, let your kids catch you reading the Bible. If you're a teacher, speak about it with awe and love.

Let's raise a generation that doesn't just know the Bible but loves it and honors it.

4. Kids Can Know The Scriptures Deeply

Spurgeon's line—"It is a good deal to say of a child that he has 'known the holy Scriptures'"—really challenged me. Because he's right: it's one thing to teach the Bible, and another for kids to really know it. To internalize it. To let it shape their worldview.

That's why I want to encourage you to raise the bar. Don't buy into the myth that kids can't understand deep truth. They can. They're sponges. They have the capacity to grasp sin, salvation, grace, repentance, and faith. Sure, we adjust our language and presentation—but never the message.

Give kids credit. And even more, believe God for big things in their spiritual development.

5. Faith Is The Key That Unlocks The Word

Here's something Spurgeon points out that I think we often miss: Scripture alone doesn't save. It prepares the heart, lays the foundation, and points to the truth—but it's faith in Jesus that brings salvation.

This is a huge reminder for us as children's ministry leaders. Our goal isn't just to help kids memorize verses or retell Bible stories. Our ultimate prayer is that they would trust in Jesus—personally, fully, and truly.

And don't get discouraged if you don't see immediate fruit. Seeds take time. Some of the children in your class or home might not have their "sunrise moment" of salvation today, but keep planting. Keep watering. Keep pointing to Jesus. He is the goal.

6. Spiritual Growth Is A Journey Of Faith

Spurgeon wraps the chapter by reminding us that even after salvation, kids grow through faith. It's not about figuring everything out or having perfect theology. It's about staying connected to Jesus and continuing to trust Him.

So as ministry leaders, let's keep feeding faith. Let's help our kids take the next step—whether that's understanding prayer, learning to forgive, sharing their faith, or resisting temptation. Let's guide them as they grow from "ABC" to "XYZ" in their walk with Jesus.

And remember: faith is not childish. It's childlike. There's a difference.

7. You Are Shaping World-Changers

Spurgeon ends with one of my favorite ideas in the whole chapter: the child in your class or your living room might be tomorrow's pastor, missionary, or ministry leader. That's not romanticism—that's reality. You don't know the future of the children you're influencing, but you're helping shape it.

So don't take your calling lightly. Whether you lead a class of 30 or tuck in one child at night with a Bible story, you are part of God's big story. You are helping kids know the Scriptures and come to saving faith in Christ. That's the most important work in the world.

Final Thoughts

Friends, we are all called to be like Lois and Eunice. Whether you're a parent, a pastor, or a volunteer—you have a role to play. Let's commit to faithfully teaching the Scriptures, modeling reverence for God's Word, and pointing every child toward Jesus.

Because when kids know the Word, trust in Jesus, and grow in faith, everything changes.

Let's raise up a generation like Timothy—and may they change the world for Christ.

~ 9 ~

WHAT DO YOU MEAN BY THIS SERVICE?

We should view everything in life through the lens of redemption—that's when we'll see things the way they really are. It makes a world of difference whether you interpret life based on human effort or from the perspective of the cross. We don't truly see anything clearly until Jesus becomes our light. When you look at the world through the filter of His sacrificial death, everything becomes clearer and more meaningful. Use the lens of the cross, and your vision will stretch far and true: see sinners through the cross, see saints through the cross, see sin through the cross, and view the joys and struggles of life through the cross. Look at heaven and hell through the cross. Notice how much emphasis was placed on the blood of the Passover lamb—and take from that how much we should emphasize the sacrifice of Jesus. In fact, we should make everything about Him, because Christ is everything.

We read in Deuteronomy, chapter six, verse eight, about the Lord's commands: "Tie them as symbols on your hands and bind them on your foreheads. Write them on the doorframes of your houses and on your gates." So we see that the law was to be written right alongside the signs of the blood. In Switzerland, in some Protestant villages, you'll still see Bible verses posted on doorframes. I kind of wish we had that tradition here in England. Imagine how much gospel could be shared with people walking by if Scripture verses were on every Christian's doorway! Some might mock it as being too showy or self-righteous, but we could deal with that. In our times, very few people could be accused of being "too religious." I personally love to see Scripture verses displayed in our homes—in every room, on the molding, and even on the walls—but especially outside, on the door. What a great way to advertise the gospel at little cost! But think of this: when the Jewish family wrote a command or promise on their doorframe, it was on wood that had been stained with the blood of a lamb. When the next Passover came, more blood was applied with a hyssop branch, right over those words. How powerful it is to picture God's law paired with the sacrifice that made it beautiful and honorable. As someone who's been redeemed, God's commands come to me in that context; His promises are made to someone who was bought with blood; His instruction reaches me as someone who's already been atoned for. When Jesus holds the law, it's not a sword to strike us down—it's a treasure to bless us. Every truth becomes more valuable when seen through the cross. Even the Bible itself becomes so much more precious when you realize it speaks to you as someone Jesus died for, with every page carrying the imprint of the hands that were nailed to the cross.

Now you can see how God did everything possible to keep the blood of the Passover lamb at the center of His people's attention. Likewise, you and I must do everything we can to keep the atoning sacrifice of Jesus front and center in people's hearts forever. Jesus was made sin for us, even though He never sinned, so that we could become the righteousness of God through Him.

Now let's think about the moment that tied the Passover directly to family life: "When your children ask you, 'What does this ceremony mean to you?' you shall answer, 'It is the Lord's Passover sacrifice.'"

We should encourage our children to be curious about God. Oh, how wonderful it would be if we could stir up their interest so they'd start asking questions about spiritual things! Some children become inquisitive early, while others seem just as indifferent as many adults. Either way, we need to engage them. It's important to explain the Lord's Supper to children since it visually represents the death of Jesus. I actually wish children had more chances to witness this ordinance. Both baptism and communion should be visible to the next generation so they can ask, "What does this mean?" Communion is a living, ongoing sermon about the gospel, centered on the sacrifice for sin. Even if some churches stop preaching about the atonement, they can't erase it from the Lord's Table. You simply can't explain the broken bread and the cup of juice without talking about Jesus' death in our place. You can't talk about "the body of Christ" without mentioning His suffering and substitution for us. So let your children see the Lord's Supper, and make sure they clearly understand what it means. And even if they can't yet see the Supper itself, keep talking to them about the cross. Take them to the garden of Gethsemane, to the judgment seat at Gabbatha, and to the hill of Golgotha. Teach them songs of sorrow and love about the One who gave His life for us. Tell them who suffered and why. Even though I'm not fond of every line in the hymn, I still want children to sing:

There is a green hill far away,
Outside a city wall.

And also:

He knew how wicked we had been,
And knew that God must punish sin;
So out of pity Jesus said,
He'd bear the punishment instead.

And once you've stirred up their interest in this amazing subject, be ready to explain how God can be perfectly just and still declare guilty people righteous. Children really can understand the message of Jesus dying in our place—it's meant to be a gospel for even the youngest hearts. The truth of substitution is simple, even though it's deep. We shouldn't rest until our children not only know this but believe it. This is essential knowledge—it unlocks everything else. If our children know the cross, they've started strong. If they understand this, they've laid a good foundation.

But to get there, you'll need to teach them that they need a Savior. You can't skip this. Don't feed them the flattering idea that they're naturally good and just need to grow into it. Tell them the truth—they need to be born again. Don't puff them up with talk about their innocence. Instead, help them see their sin. Talk about the specific ways children are prone to sin, and ask the Holy Spirit to convict their hearts. Speak to children as honestly as you would to adults. Don't be shallow with them—half-truths don't help anyone, young or old. These boys and girls need forgiveness through the blood of Jesus just like the rest of us. Don't hesitate to tell them they're lost without Him, or they won't see why they need Him. Let them know sin has consequences—and warn them sincerely. Be gentle, but be truthful. Don't hide the reality of judgment from them just because they're young. Once they're old enough to understand right from wrong, they are responsible. And if they don't believe in Jesus, they'll be judged on the last day. Show them what it means to stand before God, and tell them they'll be held accountable. Do everything you can to awaken their conscience—and ask the Holy Spirit to work through you until their hearts soften and they recognize their need for salvation.

Children need the message of the cross so they can be saved now. I thank God that in our Sunday School, we believe that kids can be saved as kids. I've had the great joy of seeing so many boys and girls profess faith in Christ. In fact, some of the clearest, most solid, and most insightful conversions I've ever seen were among children. Rather than being less grounded, they often know Scripture and the doctrines of grace better than adults. So many of these children have spoken about the things of God with joy in their hearts and strong understanding. Keep going, teachers. Believe that God will save your students. Don't settle for simply planting seeds that might grow years down the road—aim for now. Expect your students to come to faith while they're still young. Pray that they won't wander into the world and return broken later—but that they'll be spared from destruction and grow up in the fold of Christ. First as lambs in His flock, then as sheep guided by His hand.

Here's something I know for sure: if we teach our children about the atonement clearly and directly, we'll grow from it ourselves. Sometimes I think God will revive His Church and bring us back to strong faith through a movement among the children. If young people began pouring into our churches, how it would stir the tired and passive to life! Kids who love Jesus help keep a church vibrant. Oh, how we need more of them! If God helps us teach children, He'll also be teaching us. There's no better way to learn something than to teach it. You don't really know a truth until you can explain it to a child. If you try to help a child grasp the atonement, your own understanding will deepen—and that's why I encourage you to take on this holy task.

What a blessing it would be if our children are firmly grounded in Christ's redeeming work! If they are protected from the false gospels of our time and taught to stand on the unshakable truth of Jesus' finished work, we can look forward to a generation that will carry on the faith—and maybe even surpass us. Your Sunday Schools are fantastic—but what's the point if the gospel isn't taught in them? You gather kids and keep them quiet for 90 minutes, then send them home. That may give parents a break, and that might be why they send them—but the real value is in what the children are taught. The most important truth should be the one we talk about most—and that is the cross. Some teachers talk about being good boys and girls. In other words, they preach law to kids even though they preach grace to adults. Is that fair? Is that wise? Kids need the full gospel—the pure gospel. They deserve it. And if the Holy Spirit is their teacher, they can grasp it as well as any adult. Tell them that Jesus died—the righteous for the unrighteous—to bring us to God. I say this with complete confidence: I trust the teachers. I've never known a more devoted group of Christian men and women. They love the Old Gospel and they love winning souls. Be encouraged—the same God who saved many of your students is going to save many more. And we'll all rejoice as we see child after child come to Christ.

Reflections from Ryan

Teaching Kids the Power of the Cross

One of the most powerful scenes in Chapter 9 is when Spurgeon paints the image of a Jewish home with Scripture written on the doorframe—written over wood stained with the blood of the Passover lamb. It's such a vivid picture: truth and grace, law and sacrifice, commandments and mercy—all held together by the crimson mark of redemption.

That's exactly what we need today as parents and children's ministry leaders. Our homes, our ministries, our classrooms, our relationships—they need to be covered in Scripture and soaked in the story of the cross.

And Spurgeon is right: everything changes when we start seeing the world through the lens of Jesus' sacrifice. When the cross becomes the filter for how we see people, problems, and even parenting, we start walking in a new kind of wisdom.

1. The Cross Should Be Central To Our Teaching

Let's be honest: it's easy to get caught up in entertaining kids. It's easy to focus on behavior. It's even easy to give moral instruction and leave it at that. "Be nice." "Tell the truth." "Don't bully others at school." And while there's a place for teaching character and behavior, our greatest calling is not behavior modification—it's gospel transformation.

The cross must be central. That doesn't mean you turn every Bible story into a Good Friday sermon—but it does mean that the life, death, and resurrection of Jesus should be the foundation behind everything we say and do. Spurgeon reminds us that the atonement isn't just another doctrine—it's the doctrine that makes everything else make sense.

As you plan your lessons or have conversations with your kids, make it your goal to tie it back to Jesus. Help them see that the Bible isn't just a collection of disconnected stories—it's one big story about redemption. Help them see that Jesus didn't just come to be an example; He came to be our substitute.

2. Make Space For Holy Curiosity

Spurgeon quotes that moment in Exodus where God tells parents: "When your children ask you, 'What do you mean by this service?'" That's such a great parenting and ministry moment. Because if we're living out a gospel-saturated life, kids will ask questions.

But are we creating space for questions? Are we sparking curiosity in their hearts?

In our ministries and homes, we should be setting up visual, emotional, and conversational cues that stir kids to wonder. Spurgeon makes a great point—our children need to see baptism and communion. When kids sit in the back row of church coloring during communion, we're missing something. Let them see it. Let them ask questions. And when they do, be ready to give them answers soaked in grace and truth.

You don't have to be a theologian to answer kids' questions. You just have to be honest, Christ-focused, and willing to admit when you don't know. Then go on the journey with them. Say, "Let's look this up together." You'll grow as much as they will.

3. Don't Hold Back The Whole Truth

I know it's tempting to sugarcoat the gospel for kids. We don't want to scare them. We don't want them having nightmares about judgment or hell. And yes, there is a tender way to talk about these things—but there's also a truthful way that should not be avoided.

Kids are capable of understanding the seriousness of sin and the beauty of grace. In fact, sometimes they grasp it more purely than adults do. When we leave out the problem, we rob them of the joy of the solution. Spurgeon is spot-on when he says, "Don't bolster [a child] up with the fancy of his own innocence."

Teach kids that they're loved beyond measure—but also that they're in need of rescue. Teach them about sin and grace. Judgment and mercy. Heaven and hell. This is not being harsh—it's being faithful.

4. Believe In The Salvation Of Children

If there's one line in this chapter I wish I could post above every KidMin classroom, it's this: "Be working for immediate conversion. Expect fruit in your children while they are children."

Let's be done with the idea that spiritual decisions are something for "later." Now is the time. God doesn't wait until a child is a teenager or adult to begin stirring their heart. He works now. He saves now.

I've seen it myself. The clearest gospel testimonies I've ever heard didn't come from seminary students. They came from 9-year-olds in our children's church. I've watched kids explain substitution and grace more clearly than adults who've sat through 500 sermons. Don't underestimate the capacity of a child to understand the gospel. The Holy Spirit doesn't wait for someone to hit a certain age before He works in their heart.

As leaders, we need to expect salvation. Pray for it. Watch for it. Guide kids through it. Follow up with them. Help them build a real, personal relationship with Jesus. And then disciple them deeply—because saved kids are still growing kids.

5. Keep The Gospel Central In Your Heart, Too

Finally, Spurgeon reminds us of something beautiful: when you teach the cross to children, it revives your own heart.

This is one of my favorite truths. I can't tell you how many times I've been in a class with kids, walking through a Bible story, and suddenly I realize—this isn't just for them. This is for me, too.

Explaining the cross to a child has a way of stripping away all the fluff. It brings you back to the simplicity and power of the gospel. It reminds you why you're doing what you're doing in the first place.

You don't truly know a truth until you can teach it to a child. And when you do, you'll fall in love with it all over again.

Final Thoughts

Let's go back to that image again: Scripture on the doorframe, covered with the blood of a lamb. That's the image I want to leave you with. As you lead, teach, and parent, write the Word of God into every moment—but never forget that it only has power because of the blood of Jesus.

Keep pointing kids to the cross. Keep expecting God to move. And keep believing that the next generation will be stronger, bolder, and more rooted in truth than the one before—because they've been grounded in the gospel.

Let's raise up a generation who don't just know about the cross—but who cling to it with everything they've got.

~ 10 ~

SAMUEL AND HIS TEACHERS

In the days of Eli, the word of the Lord was rare, and there were no regular visions. So when God finally did speak, it was a big deal that at least one chosen person had both the ears to hear and the heart to obey. Eli failed to train his own sons to be willing servants and attentive listeners to God's word. He couldn't use the excuse of being incapable, because he did succeed in raising young Samuel to listen respectfully to God. Oh, how important it is that those who care deeply about others' souls would pay just as much attention to their own families. Poor Eli, like many today, you were made a caretaker of other people's vineyards, but you didn't care for your own. Every time he looked at the godly child Samuel, his heart must have hurt. When he thought about his own sons—neglected, undisciplined, and openly corrupt—Samuel stood as living proof of what God's grace can do when a child is raised in reverence for God. On the other hand, Hophni and Phinehas were a sad example of what happens when even good men are too indulgent with their kids. Oh Eli, if only you had been as diligent with your own sons as you were with Hannah's son, they wouldn't have grown into such wicked men. Israel wouldn't have hated the Lord's offering because of the sexual sin these corrupt priests were committing right outside the tabernacle. May God give us grace to raise our children in a way that they will recognize His voice when He calls.

Samuel was blessed with a godly father—and even more importantly, with a deeply devoted mother. Hannah was a woman with poetic talent, as shown in her powerful song: "My heart rejoices in the Lord; my strength is lifted up by the Lord. I can speak boldly against my enemies because I rejoice in Your salvation." Every line of that song is filled with poetic beauty, strength, and humility. Even Mary, the mother of Jesus, used similar language in her own song. More importantly, Hannah was a woman of prayer. She had once been filled with sorrow, but her prayers came back to her as blessings. God gave her a son, and that child was incredibly precious to her. To show her gratitude—and to fulfill a vow she had made in her sorrow—she gave God the best thing she had: she brought her son to the Lord in Shiloh. This is a powerful reminder to all godly parents to dedicate their children to God. What a blessing it would be if our kids were all like Isaac— children of the promise! How happy we'd be if our children all grew up to worship the Redeemer! Some of you have experienced this—you've seen all your children come to faith in Jesus. Every one of your treasures now belongs to God. When they were young, you dedicated them to the Lord in prayer—and now God has answered. I love it when families have a little celebration at home when a new child is born. It's good for friends and family to gather in prayer, asking that the child will inherit God's promises, come to faith early in life, and join God's family.

You'll notice that since Samuel was placed under Eli's care, Eli had taught him some basics of faith. But it seems he hadn't explained the unique way God sometimes reveals Himself to prophets—probably never imagining that Samuel would one day receive such a calling. On that unforgettable night, just before dawn, when the lamp of God was about to go out, the Lord called, "Samuel, Samuel." The young boy didn't recognize that it was God's voice—he thought it was just a person speaking, because he had never been taught to expect God to speak like that. But the fact that Samuel responded right away shows that he had already learned the heart of true religion: obedience. That habit of obeying helped him in that confusing moment. He ran to Eli and said, "Here I am, you called me." Even though this happened three times, he didn't hesitate to get up from his warm bed and run to his guardian—maybe thinking the old man needed something during the night. This is proof that Samuel had developed a good foundation of obedience, even though he didn't yet understand the mystery of God's call. It's far better to train a young heart to obey than to fill a child's mind with head knowledge, no matter how valuable that knowledge is. An ounce of obedience is worth more than a ton of learning.

Once Eli realized that God was calling the boy, he taught Samuel his very first little prayer. It was short, but powerful: "Speak, Lord, for Your servant is listening." Every Christian parent should explain what prayer is to their child—tell them that God hears and answers, point them to Jesus, and then encourage them to speak to God in their own words, morning and night. Gather the children around you, listen to their prayers, help them know what to say, and remind them of God's promises. You'll be amazed—and sometimes amused—by what they say. But more often than not, you'll be moved by the honesty of their words, their confessions, and their heartfelt requests. I'm convinced that if any Christian overheard a little child praying sincerely, they would never again want to teach a memorized prayer. They'd realize that spontaneous prayer is far better for shaping a child's heart than even the best-written form—and that the memorized forms should be set aside altogether. Still, I don't want to be too harsh. If you must teach a set prayer, at least make sure it's honest. Don't teach a child to say anything that isn't true. If you use a catechism, make sure it lines up with Scripture. Otherwise, you're training them to speak falsehoods. Only teach them the truth of Jesus, as much as they're able to understand it—and pray that the Holy Spirit will write that truth on their hearts. It's better to give no direction at all than to give misleading ones. A fake signal is worse than no signal. If you teach kids to say things that aren't truly theirs, especially in spiritual matters, you're doing more harm than atheism ever could. Fake religion is one of the greatest enemies of real faith. So if you must use a catechism or a memorized prayer, make sure it's true—and don't put words into a child's mouth that they wouldn't honestly say from their own heart.

We also need to be more careful about truthfulness in general. If a child says he saw something from a window but it was actually from the door, correct him gently and make him retell it accurately. This teaches the value of complete honesty. And especially when it comes to spiritual matters, don't rush your child into participating in things they're not ready for. Don't encourage them to take Communion unless you genuinely believe there's a real work of grace in their life. Why let them take part in something so sacred if they're not spiritually prepared? Make sure your child knows that religion is a serious matter—it's not something to play with or fake. Help them understand that nothing is more offensive to God than hypocrisy. Don't let your little Samuel become a little hypocrite. Instead, raise your precious child to speak to God with a serious heart and a clear conscience. Don't let them say anything in a catechism answer or a memorized prayer unless it's really true for them. And if you must use a set prayer, make sure it reflects the real thoughts and needs of a child.

It's been said about Rev. John Angell James: "Like many of the great and honored leaders in the Church, he had a godly mother who would take her children one by one into her room and pray with them individually for their salvation. This act, which fulfilled her own spiritual duty, helped shape her children's character—and most, if not all, of them grew up to honor her." When have such efforts ever failed? I urge all Sunday school teachers—though many of you already do this—to encourage spiritual interest in children as soon as you see even the smallest sign of it. Believe that children can be truly converted as children. Believe that God can reach their hearts, save them, and welcome them into His family even before they become adults.

Reflections from Ryan

Raising Modern Samuels in a Noisy World

There's something powerful about rereading the story of young Samuel through the lens of Charles Spurgeon. The truth is, not much has changed since the days of Eli. God is still speaking, but many people—kids and adults alike—aren't trained to listen. The noise of the world is louder than ever. Screens, schedules, sports, and social media all compete for our kids' attention. So what do we do? We do what Hannah did. What Eli should have done with his own boys. We do the slow, faithful work of raising kids to recognize and respond to the voice of God.

Samuel's story reminds me that spiritual sensitivity doesn't happen by accident. It happens when we—as parents, pastors, and KidMin leaders—intentionally create space for it. That starts with the atmosphere we build in our homes and ministries. Spurgeon nailed it when he said, "An ounce of obedience is better than a ton of learning." In today's culture, we're tempted to believe that filling our kids' heads with information—Bible facts, memory verses, polished prayers—is the goal. But the real goal? Raising kids who obey God when no one's looking. Kids who run toward God's voice when they hear it, even if they don't fully understand what it is yet.

Let me offer three takeaways that I believe are mission-critical for every children's ministry leader and every parent reading this.

1. Start With The Heart, Not Just The Head

We've got to stop measuring discipleship by how much a child knows, and start measuring it by how much they obey. Yes, Bible literacy is important. But if we want our kids to follow Jesus for a lifetime, we need to disciple their hearts, not just their minds.

Samuel didn't know God's voice yet, but he had learned the discipline of obedience. He didn't argue. He didn't hesitate. He just ran to Eli every time he thought he was needed. That kind of heart posture is learned through consistent modeling. It's built through trust and nurture. In your ministry or home, ask yourself: Am I raising kids who are eager to say yes to God? Do I give them chances to practice obedience, not just knowledge?

Create moments where children learn to listen. Keep it simple: give them a quiet moment during worship to ask, "God, is there anything You want to say to me today?" It might be awkward at first. That's okay. Learning to listen to God is a skill—just like prayer, just like kindness. It has to be taught and practiced.

2. Let Prayer Be Personal, Not Just Polished

I love how Spurgeon challenged parents to let their kids pray with their own words. He said something that should shake us up: "Don't put into a child's mouth a word which the child cannot truly say from his heart." Ouch. How often do we hand kids a script and call it prayer? How often do we teach them to recite instead of relate?

Teaching children to pray from their hearts is one of the most powerful things we can do. It doesn't have to be complicated. It starts by asking them questions like, "What do you want to thank God for today?" or "Is there anything you're worried about that we can ask God to help with?" Then let them pray in their own way. They might fumble through it. They might giggle. They might go silent. That's okay. You're creating a safe space for them to encounter God—not just learn about Him.

Parents: put your phone down, gather your family, and have simple moments of prayer together. Ministry leaders: create space in your programs for unstructured prayer. Train your volunteers to pray with children, not just for them. There is no junior Holy Spirit. God loves hearing the voices of children, just as they are.

3. Don't Just Dedicate Your Children—Disciple Them

I've seen a lot of baby dedications over the years. They're beautiful, emotional, and full of promise. But let's be honest: what happens after the dedication? Spurgeon pointed out that Hannah didn't just dedicate Samuel—she gave him to the Lord in every way. Her follow-through was as powerful as her initial promise.

Our kids don't become devoted followers of Christ just because we brought them to church or signed a commitment card. It happens because we, like Hannah, make intentional, costly choices day after day to lead them to the feet of Jesus. That means showing up to church when we're tired. That means talking about God around the dinner table. That means addressing sin with grace and truth. That means modeling the kind of faith we want them to live out.

In your church, don't let child dedications be a photo op. Let them be a launching point for a partnership between the church and the home. Walk with those parents. Resource them. Pray for them. Let's not just dedicate children—we must disciple them, one step at a time.

Final Thoughts
Don't Raise Little Hypocrites

That might sound harsh, but Spurgeon said it before I did. And I think he's right. We live in a culture where children are often praised for "looking spiritual" rather than being spiritual. But fake religion is more dangerous than no religion. Our kids don't need to know how to act holy—they need to know how to walk with a holy God.

Let's not raise little Samuels who know all the right words but none of the right heart. Let's raise children who say, "Speak, Lord, Your servant is listening"—and actually mean it.

As you serve, as you parent, as you teach, remember: Samuel didn't become a mighty prophet overnight. He became one because of a praying mother, a faithful mentor, and a God who calls children by name.

You may never be famous. Your ministry may never go viral. But if you faithfully raise one child to recognize the voice of God and obey it, you have succeeded in the highest calling on earth.

Let's raise a generation who hears the voice of the Lord and says, "Here I am."

~ 11 ~

INSTRUCTIONS FOR TEACHERS AND PARENTS

First, get the kids to come to your class. Some teachers complain that they just can't find students. In London, we've started going door-to-door to reach children—and that's a great idea. Every small town and village should do the same. Get every child you can into Sunday school. My advice is this: do everything fair and right to bring the kids in. But don't bribe them. That's something we strongly oppose. Bribing is only done in the lowest types of schools—schools so poor that even the kids' own parents are too wise to send them there.

"But Farmer Brown won't hire them unless they go," or "the landowner will fire them," or "if the kids don't go to church school on Sundays, they're not allowed to come during the week." That kind of pathetic bribery needs to stop. It just shows how weak, desperate, and shameful a group is when they have to rely on such a shallow tactic to get people in.

Except for that one method—don't be too picky about how you get kids to come to school. If I couldn't get people to come hear me preach in a black suit, I'd wear a uniform tomorrow. I'd do whatever it took to fill the seats. Better to try something unusual than preach to an empty church or teach in an empty classroom.

When I was in Scotland, we hired a town crier to walk through the village inviting people to come. And it worked! Use every appropriate method—but make sure you get the kids in. I know pastors who've gone out into the streets on Sunday afternoons and talked to kids playing outside, convincing them to come inside. That's what a dedicated teacher does. He'll say, "Hey John, come join us at Sunday school. You'll love it!" Then he brings them in and, with a kind and welcoming spirit, tells stories about kids who loved Jesus. That's how the classroom fills up. Go out and bring them in. There's no law against it—and in this battle against the enemy, anything fair is allowed.

So, first step: get the kids—and get them however you can.

Next, get the kids to like you. "Come, children, listen to me." You remember how school used to be when we stood stiffly with our hands behind our backs reciting lessons. But that wasn't David's way. His approach was, "Come here, children—come sit close." The child thinks, "Wow, what a nice teacher—one who invites me in, not one who says 'Go away.'"

The problem with many teachers is that they keep too much distance between themselves and their students, creating a kind of cold respect. But if you really want to teach children, you've got to first win their hearts with kindness. Say, "Come, children."

We've known some good men who, sadly, kids wanted nothing to do with. Remember the story of the two little boys who were asked if they wanted to go to Heaven? To the teacher's shock, they said, "Not really." When asked why, one said, "Because Grandpa would be there—and he'd just yell, 'Get out of here, boys!' I wouldn't want to spend eternity with Grandpa."

So if a kid's teacher talks about Jesus but always looks grumpy, what do you think the kid assumes? "Is Jesus like you? If He is, I don't think I want Him."

And then there's the teacher who slaps a kid's ear when they're slightly annoyed—but also tells them they should be kind and forgiving. The kid thinks, "That sounds nice, but you sure don't show me how."

If you push a kid away, you lose your influence. You won't be able to teach them anything. It's pointless to try teaching someone who doesn't even like you—so focus on earning their love. Once you've done that, they'll learn anything from you.

Next, get their attention. "Come, children, listen to me." If they aren't listening, your words won't make any difference. Without their attention, your teaching becomes dull for both you and the kids. You simply can't teach if they're not tuned in.

"That's exactly my problem," you might say. Well, it depends on what you're giving them. If it's worth paying attention to, they'll listen. Give them something valuable and interesting, and you'll capture their attention.

It's not true for every kid in every situation, but it's almost always the case. And don't forget to tell them stories. Critics may dislike hearing stories in sermons, but some of us know better—we know what wakes up a room. From experience, we know a few stories here and there are perfect for grabbing the attention of people who'd otherwise tune out of dry lectures.

Try to collect interesting illustrations throughout your week. If you're a smart teacher, you'll always find something to turn into a story for your students. When they start getting bored, say, "Do you know the Five Bells?"—if that's a place in town, they'll perk up. Or ask, "Do you know the road by the Red Lion?" Then share something you've read or heard that will pull their attention back to the lesson.

One little girl once said, "Daddy, I like hearing Pastor So-and-so preach because he uses so many 'likes'—'like this' and 'like that.'" Yes, kids love those kinds of comparisons.

Create parables, draw word pictures, use examples—and your teaching will connect. Honestly, if I were a kid sitting in your class, and you didn't tell me a story every now and then, you'd probably see the back of my head more than my face. If the room were hot, my head would start to nod, and I'd probably fall asleep or start messing around with my friend Tom. I'd do all sorts of things—unless you made the effort to keep me interested.

So remember, make sure your kids listen.

Reflections from Ryan

Winning the Heart of a Child Today

Charles Spurgeon's wisdom in this chapter couldn't be more relevant today. While children's ministry may look different now than it did in the 1800s, the heart of what he's saying remains true: if we want to impact kids for Jesus, we have to get them in the room, win their hearts, and keep their attention. This is foundational to both parenting and children's ministry.

Let's start with the first challenge: get the children to come.

This might seem like a no-brainer, but in an age of screen time, sports leagues, fractured family schedules, and competing commitments, getting kids to consistently show up to church or faith-based programming is no small feat. But hear me on this: it's worth every ounce of effort.

We've got to stop thinking, "If we build it, they will come," and start thinking like missionaries. Spurgeon talks about going out into the streets and inviting children in—and today, that might mean showing up at school events, being present at community festivals, running outreach nights, or being active on social media where parents are scrolling. If we want to disciple kids, we have to meet them where they are—then lovingly guide them toward where they need to be.

And don't worry about using creative strategies. Spurgeon said if a black coat didn't bring people into his chapel, he'd wear a uniform! His point? Don't let pride or tradition keep you from being effective. If handing out popsicles in the park or using a silly costume gets a kid to step through your church doors—go for it. Spurgeon draws the line at bribery, and so should we. But creativity, relevance, and persistence? Those are tools of a faithful teacher.

Second, get them to love you. This one hits home.

If you're in children's ministry—or raising kids—you already know that kids don't learn well from people they don't like. Trust and relationship are the bridges over which truth travels. If a child sees you as distant, distracted, or disinterested, they'll tune you out, no matter how solid your content is. But if you take the time to learn their name, ask about their dog, show up to their soccer game, or simply get down on their level and smile—they'll open up. And when their heart opens, you've got a doorway for discipleship.

I love how Spurgeon paints the picture of David saying, "Come, children." It's warm. It's invitational. It's personal. And it's how Jesus modeled ministry, too. He didn't wave from a distance—He drew close, He sat with children, and He blessed them. As leaders and parents, we need to ask ourselves: Do kids feel welcomed by us? Do they feel seen, safe, and wanted?

It's possible to teach kids all the right facts about God, but if they don't see the love of God through you, it won't stick. One of the greatest ways you can point a child to Jesus is by being someone they love to be around.

And that leads into the third point: get their attention.

We live in the most distracted generation in history. Kids are surrounded by entertainment options that are fast, flashy, and full of stimulation. You can fight against it—or you can learn from it.

Spurgeon understood this. That's why he talks about using stories, illustrations, and real-life examples to keep kids engaged. And he wasn't afraid of being criticized for it, either. He knew that if the goal is to capture a child's attention long enough to teach them truth, it's worth telling a few good stories.

In our culture today, this might mean using video clips, funny props, games, or pop culture references. It might mean breaking up your lesson into 3-minute sections instead of 20-minute lectures. It might mean changing how you use your classroom space, or how you transition between activities. Whatever you do, make it intentional. A bored child is a disengaged child—and disengaged kids rarely absorb spiritual truth.

At the same time, we don't have to put on a circus. What kids are hungry for—more than lights and sounds—is something real. They want someone to look them in the eyes and say, "God made you. He loves you. He's got a purpose for your life." You don't need to be cool to get their attention—you need to be authentic. You need to be present. And when you pair that authenticity with a little creativity? That's where the magic happens.

Let me also encourage you, especially if you're a volunteer teacher or a parent who's doing your best and feels a bit overwhelmed: you don't have to do this alone. We are the Body of Christ. Lean on your team. Share ideas. Pray with each other. If you're a children's pastor, equip your volunteers with stories, training, and tools to help them engage. If you're a parent, talk with other parents about what works in your home. Community makes us stronger.

Here's a quick list of practical takeaways based on Spurgeon's chapter and what I've learned over the years:

1. **Be intentional about outreach.** Make a plan to reach kids who aren't coming—whether through your local school, community center, or neighborhood block parties

2. **Don't be afraid to try new things.** Use creativity, but stay grounded in the gospel. The message never changes, but the methods can.

3. **Build relationships before teaching lessons.** Trust opens the door to transformation.

4. **Get down on their level—literally and emotionally.** Sit on the floor, ask questions, and listen to kids.

5. **Use stories often.** They work—Jesus used them, Spurgeon used them, and so should we.

6. **Make it fun, but make it matter.** Kids should laugh, play, and enjoy church—but always walk away knowing Jesus loves them.

7. **Stay consistent.** Trust and attention are built over time. Keep showing up. Keep loving them. Keep planting seeds.

At the end of the day, this work we do with children isn't about running programs or filling seats. It's about eternity. Every single child you reach is a soul that matters to God. Spurgeon knew that. That's why he was so passionate about these principles. And that's why we should be, too.

So let's go get the kids. Let's win their hearts. Let's keep their attention. And let's point them to Jesus—because there's no greater calling.

~ 12 ~

MODEL LESSON FOR TEACHERS

Teach them to live morally: "Keep your tongue from evil, and your lips from telling lies. Turn away from wrongdoing, and do good; seek peace, and go after it." Now, we never teach morality as the path to salvation. God forbid that we would ever mix human works into the salvation that comes through Christ Jesus! "By grace you have been saved through faith, and that not from yourselves, it is the gift of God." Still, we do teach morality while we also teach spiritual truth; and I've always found that the gospel produces the best moral behavior in the world. I want every Sunday school teacher to care about the behavior of the boys and girls they teach, and to speak directly about the sins that are most common in young people. A teacher can honestly and helpfully say many things to their class that others wouldn't be able to say— especially when it comes to warning them about lying (a common issue with children), stealing small things, disrespecting their parents, or not honoring the Lord's Day. I want teachers to call out these sins clearly and specifically. It's not helpful to talk about sin in general terms—you have to deal with them one at a time, like David did. Start with the mouth: "Keep your tongue from evil, and your lips from telling lies." Then focus on their behavior: "Turn away from evil, and do good; seek peace, and go after it." Even if a child's soul isn't saved by the rest of the teaching, this kind of instruction can still have a good effect on their life, and that is valuable. But morality by itself is not enough.

The best part of what we teach is godliness. I didn't say "religion," but godliness. Lots of people are religious on the outside without being godly on the inside. They go through the motions of worship, attend church, read spiritual books—but they never really think about God. Anyone who doesn't honor God, pray to Him, or love Him is not a godly person, no matter how religious they may look. Work hard to teach every child to keep their eyes on God. Burn into their memory these words: "You, God, see me." Help them remember that everything they do and think is in full view of God. No Sunday school teacher is truly doing their job unless they're constantly reminding their students that there is a God who sees and knows everything. Oh, how much better off we'd be if we ourselves were more godly—if we talked more about godliness, and if we loved godliness more!

The third lesson is about the seriousness of sin. If a child doesn't learn this, they'll never understand the way to Heaven. None of us really knew what a Savior Jesus is until we first realized how awful sin is. If the Holy Spirit doesn't show us just how terrible sin truly is, we'll never fully grasp how wonderful salvation is. So let's ask for His help when we teach, so we can clearly show how disgusting and destructive sin really is. "The face of the Lord is against those who do evil, to erase their memory from the earth." Don't go easy on your children when it comes to this—let them see where sin leads. Don't be like those who are too scared to speak plainly and honestly about sin's consequences. I once heard of a father whose son—a very rebellious young man—died suddenly.

Instead of saying to the family, as some might, "We hope your brother is in Heaven," this father, moved by God's grace, gathered his children and said, "My sons and daughters, your brother is gone, and I fear he's in hell. You knew his lifestyle. You saw how he lived. Now God has taken him in the midst of his sin." He then warned them about the reality of hell, urging them to turn away from sin and escape God's judgment. His honesty led his children to take spiritual matters seriously. But what if he had said, out of emotion and misplaced kindness, that he hoped the son went to Heaven? What would the others have thought? Probably this: "If he made it to Heaven, then we don't need to worry—we can live however we want." No, absolutely not. I believe it's not wrong to say that some people have gone to hell when their lives clearly showed they were heading there. People might ask, "Who are you to judge others?" I'm not judging them—I'm just seeing the fruit of their lives. They've already judged themselves. Their sins have gone ahead to judgment, and I have no doubt the rest will follow. "But couldn't they be saved at the last minute?" Maybe one person was—but I don't know of another, and I'm not sure there ever will be. Be honest with your children, and with God's help, teach them that "evil will destroy the wicked."

But even that isn't enough unless you teach the fourth lesson: the absolute necessity of a changed heart. "The Lord is near to those who have a broken heart, and saves those who have a contrite spirit." May God help us to constantly remind the children we teach that they must have a broken and humble heart. Good deeds won't save them without a new heart. Even the most dedicated efforts and heartfelt prayers mean nothing without deep, sincere repentance and a complete turning away from sin through God's grace and mercy. Whatever else you leave out, don't forget to teach the children the three R's: Ruin, Redemption, and Regeneration.

Tell them they are ruined by the Fall, that salvation comes only by being redeemed through the blood of Jesus Christ, and that they must be made new by the Holy Spirit. Keep these core truths front and center, and then you'll get to share the joy of the final lesson.

Fifth, tell the children about the joy and blessing of being a Christian. "The Lord redeems the life of His servants: and none of those who trust in Him will be left alone." I don't need to tell you how to talk about this subject—if you're truly a Christian, you'll never run out of things to say. When we start talking about this, it's hard to stop. Honestly, we'd rather just soak in the joy of it. How true are the words: "Blessed is the one whose sin is forgiven." "Blessed is the one who puts their trust in the Lord." Yes—blessed is the man, woman, or child who trusts in Jesus Christ and places their hope in Him. Make sure your students understand this: that the people of God—the ones bought by Christ's blood and rescued by His power—are blessed, both now and forever in Heaven. Let the children see that you are part of this blessed family. If you're going through hardship, still try to come to class with a joyful heart, so your students can say, "Our teacher is truly blessed, even though he's carrying heavy burdens." Try to always bring a cheerful spirit, so your kids will know that your faith is real and life-giving. Let this be a major focus of your teaching: that although "the righteous face many troubles," still "the Lord delivers them from them all. He protects all their bones—not one of them is broken… The Lord redeems the lives of His servants, and none who trust in Him will be left alone."

I've now shared five lessons with you. Let me end with a serious reminder: no matter how much teaching you give to your children, you must always remember that you cannot save them. Only God can do that—from beginning to end. You are simply the pen; God is the writer. You are just a sword; God is the warrior who defeats the child's sin. Always remember—you must first be taught by God yourself, and then you must pray that God will use you to teach others. Without the help of the Holy Spirit, all your effort is worthless, and the child will remain lost. It's not your teaching that saves them; it's the Spirit of God blessing your work. May He bless you with great success! He certainly will, if you are persistent in prayer and faithful in seeking Him. No sincere teacher or preacher ever "worked in vain for the Lord." Often, the bread cast on the waters has been found again after many days.

Reflections from Ryan

Teaching That Transforms

Charles Spurgeon's wisdom in this chapter may have been written over a century ago, but it reads like it was crafted for children's ministry leaders and parents today. The heart of what he's saying is this: teaching kids is about so much more than facts, behavior, and religion. It's about shaping hearts, confronting sin, and introducing them to a real, living relationship with God.

Let me walk through these five lessons and share how we can live them out today.

1. Teach Morality, But Keep The Gospel Central

Spurgeon made it clear that morality isn't the same as salvation—and yet it matters. In today's world, children are being shaped by hundreds of influences: screens, friends, social media, and the culture at large. If we're not intentional about calling out specific wrong behaviors and pointing toward right living, the world will do the teaching for us—and it won't be godly.

As ministry leaders, we shouldn't be afraid to talk to kids about lying, cheating, stealing, disobedience, or disrespect. It's okay to name the sin and explain why it's a problem. But we do this in the context of grace. We tell them what's right, but we never make them believe that "being good" is the path to Heaven. We point them to Jesus every time.

Parents—don't let "being a good kid" become the ultimate goal. Instead, make it clear that morality flows from knowing and loving Jesus. If your child tells the truth or honors their teacher, celebrate it! But always connect that behavior back to the heart. Remind them that we want to obey because we love Jesus and want to reflect Him.

2. Teach Godliness, Not Just Religion

Spurgeon hits this one hard, and I think we need to hear it just as strongly today. There is no shortage of kids in churches who can rattle off Bible stories and memory verses, but who have no idea what it means to walk with God. That's what he's warning against.

Religion without relationship is empty. It's lifeless. And our kids are smart enough to see through it. They know when we're just "playing church."

That's why I want to challenge every leader and parent reading this: don't just teach your kids about God—teach them to know Him. Help them pray real prayers. Let them see you reading your Bible—not as a performance, but as a lifeline. Model what it looks like to walk with God through joy and pain. Talk about how God is working in your life, how you hear from Him, how you trust Him. Kids don't need more "church stuff." They need godliness modeled in front of them.

3. Teach The Seriousness Of Sin

This isn't a popular topic today. In fact, even in the church, it's become easy to soften sin. We want to avoid making kids feel bad. But Spurgeon reminds us that if we skip over sin, we also skip over the Savior.

Children need to know that sin is serious. It separates us from God. It brings pain, destruction, and death. And yes, if left undealt with, it leads to eternal judgment. We don't teach that to scare kids—we teach it because it's true, and because it helps them understand how amazing grace really is.

I want to encourage you to be lovingly honest with your kids—whether in your home or your classroom. Don't minimize sin. Call it what it is. Talk about consequences. Share stories of people in Scripture (and even from your life) who experienced both the pain of sin and the hope of redemption. We're not helping our kids when we sugarcoat the gospel—we're actually robbing them of it.

4. Teach The Need For A Changed Heart

This one might be the most important of all. We live in a world obsessed with external fixes. "If I just follow the rules… say the prayer… act the part…" But the Bible is clear—what God wants most is a new heart.

There is no salvation without repentance. No life change without regeneration. No lasting fruit without a transformed heart. That's why we have to teach our kids that being a Christian isn't about doing more—it's about becoming someone new.

Ministry leaders, make sure you are pointing your kids to the work of the Holy Spirit. Don't just ask them to "try harder"—ask them to invite Jesus to change their hearts. Parents, when you discipline your child, don't stop at the behavior. Use that moment to talk about the heart behind it. Ask questions like: "Why do you think you did that?" or "What do you think God wants you to learn from this?"

We must keep the "three R's" front and center: Ruin (we are broken by sin), Redemption (Jesus paid the price), and Regeneration (we must be born again). This is the gospel. And it's the best gift we can give the next generation.

5. Teach The Joy Of Knowing Jesus

This might be my favorite point in the whole chapter. Because while we talk about sin and salvation, Spurgeon doesn't forget to end on joy. And friends, our kids need to see that following Jesus is the best thing in the world.

Too many children grow up thinking that Christianity is just a list of rules—or worse, a boring routine. Let's show them it's a relationship full of joy, peace, hope, and purpose.

Laugh with your kids. Celebrate answered prayer. Talk about the goodness of God. Let your class or your home be filled with the blessing of walking with Jesus. If they see that being a Christian is truly the best life they can live—because it's life with Jesus—they will be drawn to Him.

And if you're going through hard times right now, don't hide it. Let your kids see how your faith holds you up. Be honest about the struggle, but don't lose your joy. That kind of authenticity will leave a deep impression on young hearts.

Final Thoughts

Spurgeon ends with a reminder we all need: you can't do this alone. None of us can save a child. We can't change their hearts. We are simply tools in the hands of the Master. But what a privilege to be used by Him!

So pray. Stay close to Jesus. Keep showing up. Keep planting seeds. And trust that God is at work—even when you can't see it yet.

I believe with all my heart that your labor is not in vain. You may not always see immediate fruit, but eternity will reveal what your faithful teaching, loving correction, and joyful witness accomplished in the lives of these kids.

Let's keep pressing on. Let's keep teaching truth. Let's keep pointing kids to Jesus.

You're not just running a class or raising a child. You're investing in a soul.

And that matters more than anything.

~ 13 ~
"COME, YE CHILDREN"— THREE WARNINGS

First, remember who you're teaching—"Come, you children." I think we should always keep our audience in mind. I don't mean that we should care if we're teaching Mr. So-and-so, Sir William this, or Lord That—because in God's eyes, titles like that mean nothing—but we should remember that we're teaching people who have souls. That means we shouldn't waste their time with anything that's not worth hearing. And when you teach in Sunday school, you're, in some ways, taking on an even greater responsibility than a pastor has. A pastor preaches to adults who can think for themselves—and if they don't like what they hear, they can choose to go somewhere else. But children don't have that choice. If you teach a child wrongly, he'll believe you. If you teach him falsehoods, he'll accept them. What you teach now will stay with him for life.

You're not planting seeds in brand-new soil—Satan has already claimed that ground—but you are planting in soil that is more ready to grow fruit now than it ever will be again. A young heart is more fertile than it will be later in life, and what you plant there is likely to stay—especially if it's harmful. If you teach something wrong, it's hard to undo. Be careful. You're starting at the very beginning—don't ruin it. Some children have been treated like little Indian children who had copper plates strapped to their foreheads to keep them from growing. Many adults today are stuck in ignorance because, as children, they were never given the chance to learn. When they grew older, they didn't care to learn anything at all. So be careful what you're doing. You're teaching children—so pay attention to what you're teaching. Poison a spring, and the entire stream is contaminated. Bend a sapling the wrong way, and the full-grown oak will still be crooked. Be warned—you're dealing with a child's soul. If you're careless, you might be ruining that soul. But if God is with you, you're preparing that soul for eternity. I give you this serious warning on behalf of every child. If it's wrong to give poison to someone dying, how much worse is it to poison a life that's just beginning? If it's bad to mislead someone at the end of life, how much worse is it to send a child down the wrong path—a path they may walk for the rest of their life?

Second, remember that you're teaching for God—"Come, you children, listen to me; I will teach you the fear of the Lord." If you were just teaching geography, it wouldn't be the end of the world if you told the kids that the North Pole was near the Equator, or that South America was next to Europe, or that England was in the middle of Africa. But you're not teaching geography or astronomy or preparing them for careers. To the best of your ability, you're teaching for God. You're saying to them, "Children, you're here to learn the Word of God. We're here to help you find salvation for your souls."

So be careful what you're doing if you claim to be teaching them for God. You can wound a child's hand if you must—but please, don't wound their heart. Say whatever you want about temporary, worldly things—but when it comes to spiritual truth, I beg you, be cautious. Be sure that what you're teaching is true—and only the truth. With that kind of responsibility, your work becomes incredibly serious. Someone working for themselves may do things however they want. But if you're working for someone else, you have to make sure they're pleased with your work. If you're working for a king, you better take your duties seriously. And if you're working for God, you should tremble at the thought of doing it wrong. Remember—if you're the person you claim to be, then you're working for God. Sadly, I fear many Sunday school teachers don't fully realize how serious that calling truly is.

Third, remember that your children need to be taught—"Come, you children, listen to me: I will teach you the fear of the Lord." This makes your work even more important. If children didn't need to be taught, I wouldn't be so passionate about making sure you teach them well. Optional tasks can be done however you want. But this job is absolutely necessary. Your child needs teaching. He was born sinful. His heart is naturally turned away from God, and he'll never know the Lord unless someone teaches him. He's not like a field with good seed hidden deep in the soil. No, his heart is already filled with bad seed. Only God can plant good seed there. And you've committed yourself to be His instrument—to scatter that seed into the child's heart.

If that seed isn't planted, the child will be lost forever. His life will be one of separation from God. And when he dies, his soul will face eternal punishment. So be careful how you teach, knowing just how urgent the situation really is. This isn't just a house fire that needs your help on the firetruck. It's not just a shipwreck where you need to grab an oar and row the lifeboat. It's something greater—a soul that will never die, calling out to you: "Come and help me." So I beg you, teach them the fear of the Lord—and only that. Be eager to say, and to say honestly, "I will teach you the fear of the Lord."

Reflections from Ryan

Three Reminders That Still Matter

Charles Spurgeon had a way of writing that hits you right between the eyes—and Chapter 13 is no exception. His challenge is bold and clear: remember who you're teaching, remember why you're teaching, and remember that kids need what you're teaching. As we reflect on these truths, let me walk with you and explore how they apply to our lives as children's ministry leaders, teachers, and parents today.

1. Remember WHO You're Teaching
"Come, you children."

We live in a time where attention is divided and priorities often shift based on urgency. But in the hustle of preparing lessons, checking attendance, and setting up rotation stations, it's easy to forget that we're not just managing a room—we're shaping souls.

Every time you stand in front of a group of kids—whether you're teaching preschoolers with a puppet or leading preteens in a small group—you're doing eternal work. You're speaking into the hearts of kids who, right now, are open to receive truth in a way they may not be again.

Spurgeon reminded us that what you plant in a child's heart will grow. That's why your words matter. Your tone matters. Your lessons matter. Even your attitude when a kid spills their drink all over your lesson plan—it all matters.

We're not dealing with blank slates. These kids are already hearing messages from the world, from culture, from media, and yes, from the enemy of their souls. The seeds you sow today can be what grounds them in truth when the storms of life hit.

So next time you're tempted to throw a lesson together last minute or to just "get through" a Sunday morning, pause and remember: these are children. They matter to God. And they need someone to care enough to teach them well.

2. Remember WHY You're Teaching
"I will teach you the fear of the Lord."

You're not just filling time until the adult service is over. You're not a babysitter. You're not a volunteer to plug a hole in the schedule. You are a messenger of God.

Spurgeon said, "Wound the child's hand if you will; but, for God's sake, do not wound his heart." That line stopped me in my tracks. How often are we careless with our influence? Maybe not intentionally, but when we teach without preparation, when we deliver half-hearted messages, or when we drift from God's Word to our own opinions, we risk spiritual injury.

Every lesson you teach is a chance to put truth into the hearts of kids who are searching for answers, longing for love, and desperately needing hope. And here's the thing: kids know when you're just going through the motions. But they also know when someone truly believes what they're saying. You don't have to be the funniest, flashiest, or most experienced leader. Just be real. Be passionate. Be faithful.

And remember—you're not doing this for yourself. You're doing this for God. It's His gospel. It's His truth. And you've been entrusted to pass it on to the next generation.

Whether you're a Sunday school teacher, a children's pastor, a small group leader, or a parent reading Bible stories at bedtime—you are doing God's work. And God takes that seriously.

3. Remember That Kids NEED What You're Teaching

Spurgeon wrote that children are not born with truth in their hearts—they need it taught. That hasn't changed. In fact, today's children are bombarded with more voices than ever before. Social media, streaming content, peers, and school curriculums are all shaping what kids believe about the world, about themselves, and about God.

If we don't intentionally teach kids the truth of God's Word, someone else will teach them something else. Silence in spiritual matters is not neutral—it creates a vacuum that will be filled by something else, often something harmful.

The message we carry isn't optional—it's urgent. You and I are planting seeds that may determine whether a child grows up knowing who they are in Christ or wandering through life feeling lost and unworthy.

Let me ask you something: What are you doing each week to prepare yourself spiritually to teach the kids God has entrusted to you? How are you making sure the curriculum you use points clearly to Jesus? Are you praying for the kids by name? Are you asking God to open their hearts? These things might not be flashy, but they are powerful. And they are necessary.

Real-Life Application

Let me break this down even further. Here's what this chapter might look like lived out in your ministry or family:

- **Take Preparation Seriously:** Don't wing your lesson. Spend time in prayer and study. Ask God what He wants to say through you this week.
- **Be Present and Engaged:** When a child walks into your class or small group, be fully present. Greet them by name. Look them in the eyes. Listen to their stories—even the ones that don't make much sense.

- **Use Words That Build:** Speak life. Affirm kids. Encourage them. Point them to truth in every conversation.
- **Protect Their Hearts:** Be careful not to shame or discourage. Yes, correct when needed—but do it with love and grace. You're building their view of who God is.
- **Keep It Simple and True:** Don't feel the need to impress. Kids don't need a seminary lecture—they need a clear and compelling picture of who Jesus is and why He matters.
- **Partner with Parents:** If you're a children's pastor or volunteer, communicate regularly with parents. Share what you're teaching. Equip them to continue the conversation at home.
- **Never Underestimate Your Influence:** You may not see the fruit right away. But one seed planted in the right soil can grow into a life that impacts generations.

Friend, this chapter is a holy reminder of the weight—and the privilege—we carry. Teaching children isn't easy, and it isn't always glamorous. But it's worth it.

When you sit down with your team this week, remind them: you're not just organizing snacks or crafts or activities. You're holding the hearts of children in your hands. And what you do matters for eternity.

Let's be faithful. Let's be intentional. Let's do everything we can to say, just like the psalmist, "I will teach you the fear of the Lord."

Let's go change some lives—one child at a time.

~ 14 ~

"Come, Ye Children" —David's Invitation

It's interesting how good people often become most aware of their responsibilities when they're in the most humbling situations. David was never in a more embarrassing position than the one that inspired this Psalm. The title reads, "A Psalm of David, when he changed his behavior before Abimelech, who drove him away, and he departed." This song was written to reflect on that moment. David had been brought before King Achish, the Abimelech of Philistia, and to escape, he pretended to be insane—acting in ways that were humiliating and clearly meant to suggest madness. He was thrown out of the palace, and like always, when someone ends up in the street like that, it's likely that a group of children gathered around him. You can read the whole story in 1 Samuel 21:10–15. Later in life, when David sang praise to God and remembered how he had become a laughingstock in front of children, it was as if he said, "Because of my foolishness in front of those kids, I've damaged how future generations will see me—so now, I'll try to make it right: 'Come, children, listen to me; I will teach you to fear the Lord.'"

It's very possible that if David had never gone through that low point, he never would have recognized this responsibility; because as far as we know, nowhere else in his Psalms does he say,

"Come, children, listen to me." With the weight of ruling cities, managing provinces, and leading a nation, he probably hadn't paid much attention to the spiritual development of young people. But now, in the lowest place a man could be, pretending to have lost his mind, David remembered something important. Successful and high-ranking believers don't always think about "the lambs." That job often falls to people like Peter—men whose pride has been broken and who now find joy in proving their love for Jesus by serving, just like when Jesus asked Peter, "Do you love Me?"

"Come, children, listen to me; I will teach you to fear the Lord." The point here is that children can be taught to fear the Lord.

People often become truly wise after being incredibly foolish. David had acted foolishly, and now he showed real wisdom; and being in that wise state, he wouldn't be saying anything silly or giving bad advice. Some claim that children can't grasp the deep truths of the Christian faith. We've even known Sunday school teachers who carefully avoid discussing the central doctrines of the gospel because they believe the kids won't understand them. Sadly, this error has even made its way into the pulpit. Some preachers say, "Yes, these doctrines are true—but they're too dangerous to teach to people, because they might misuse them." That kind of thinking is nothing more than modern-day priestcraft! If God has revealed a truth, it should be preached. And even if I don't fully understand it, I'll still believe it and share it. I believe that there is no doctrine in God's Word that a child—if that child is able to be saved—is not also able to receive. I want kids to be taught all the major truths of Scripture, with no exceptions, so they can hold on to them as they grow up.

I know from experience that children can understand Scripture. As a young boy, I could discuss all kinds of tough theological topics, just from listening to conversations among my father's friends. In fact, there are some things that children seem to understand more easily at an early age than we do later in life. Kids naturally have a simplicity of faith—and that kind of faith is closely related to deep wisdom. Really, there's not much difference between the simple faith of a child and the insight of the most brilliant mind. A person who believes with childlike faith often grasps spiritual truths in a way that someone who tries to dissect everything logically never will. If you want proof that kids can be taught the truth, look at the many children in our churches and in godly homes—not extraordinary prodigies, just regular kids—like Timothy, like Samuel, and young girls too, who have come to know Jesus' love early in life. As soon as a child is capable of being lost, that child is also capable of being saved. As soon as a child can sin, that child, by the grace of God, can also believe and accept His Word. As soon as children can start picking up bad behavior, you can be sure that, under the Holy Spirit's guidance, they can learn what's good. Never go into your class assuming the children won't understand. If they don't, it might be because you don't fully understand what you're teaching. If you can't communicate clearly, maybe you're not ready for the task. You need to find simpler words, better suited to their level, and then you'll realize that the issue wasn't the children—it was the teacher.

I firmly believe that children can be saved. The same God who, in His sovereignty, calls elderly sinners out of their long life of sin, can just as easily turn a young child away from their early faults. The God who finds idle workers at the eleventh hour and sends them into the vineyard can also call young ones at sunrise to serve Him. The God who can redirect a mighty river that's been flowing for years can also shape the tiny stream just starting from its source—and direct it however He chooses. God can do anything.

He can work in the hearts of children as He sees fit, because all hearts are under His control.

I won't take more time trying to prove this point, because I trust no one is foolish enough to deny it. Still, even though you believe it, I fear many of you don't really expect to see children get saved. In many churches, there's an unfortunate hesitancy around childlike faith. People feel awkward at the thought of a little boy loving Jesus. If a little girl shows signs of following Christ, they say, "It's just a phase—it'll pass." Please, never look at a child's faith with suspicion. It's like a delicate flower—don't crush it. I once heard a story, and I believe it's true, about a little girl, maybe five or six years old, who sincerely loved Jesus and asked her mother if she could join the church. The mother told her she was too young, and the little girl was heartbroken. Eventually, the mother—seeing how genuine her daughter's faith was—spoke to the pastor. He met with the child and later told the mother, "I'm absolutely convinced she knows the Lord, but I can't let her join the church—she's just too young." When the girl heard that, a deep sadness came over her. The next morning, her mother found her in bed—with tears still in her eyes—she had died from grief. Her heart was broken because she couldn't follow her Savior and do what He asked. I wouldn't have crushed that child's spirit for anything in the world!

Be very careful how you treat young believers. Be gentle with them. Believe that children can be saved just like you can. I absolutely believe in the salvation of children. When you see a young heart turn to Jesus, don't respond with cold words or skepticism. Sometimes, it's better to be mistaken than to risk discouraging one of these little ones who believe in Christ. May God give His people a deep and lasting conviction that these tender young buds of grace deserve our greatest care.

Reflections from Ryan

The Spiritual Potential of a Child

Charles Spurgeon's message in this chapter is both bold and deeply tender. He calls out a truth that we sometimes tiptoe around: children are not just capable of following Jesus—they are invited to. And they are capable of understanding more than we often give them credit for. As leaders and parents, we need to grab hold of this truth and run with it.

Let me say it clearly: children's ministry is not babysitting. It's not spiritual entertainment. It's real ministry. Eternal ministry.

In Psalm 34:11, David says, "Come, children, listen to me; I will teach you the fear of the Lord." He's not offering a coloring sheet and a snack. He's offering a spiritual foundation that will anchor their lives. He's teaching children the fear (the reverence, the awe) of the Lord.

How often do we take that responsibility seriously?

1. You Don't Have To Wait Until They're "Old Enough"

One of the most damaging ideas we've adopted in the Church is that kids will eventually grow into their faith when they're older. That sounds harmless, but it's not what Scripture shows us. If children can be lost, then they can be saved. If they can sin, they can repent. If they can love their parents, they can love their Savior.

Jesus Himself said, "Let the little children come to Me, and do not hinder them." That wasn't symbolic. It wasn't a sermon illustration. It was an actual command. And what Spurgeon gets so right is that we hinder kids spiritually when we assume they can't really get it.

We teach kids math and science and sports strategies by the time they're five or six. We should be teaching them the deep truths of the faith with just as much intentionality.

2. Teach Big Truths With Simple Words

There's a big difference between watering down the truth and breaking it down so kids can understand it.

Spurgeon challenges us here: if we think kids can't understand what we're saying, maybe it's not the kids who are the problem—it's us. He reminds teachers and parents alike to do the hard work of making the message of the gospel clear and accessible.

If a child doesn't understand the word justification, explain it as "God making us right with Him because of Jesus." Don't avoid the topic. Don't leave the gospel on the shelf until kids hit middle school. Start now—today.

I like to say: if you can explain it to a first grader, you can explain it to anyone.

3. Don't Discourage Tender Faith

This part of Spurgeon's chapter absolutely wrecks me: the story of the little girl who wanted to join the church, but was turned away for being "too young"—and then died from heartbreak.

Whether or not that particular story was embellished over time, the truth behind it is real. We've all seen it—kids whose faith is sincere, whose love for Jesus is genuine, only to have it dismissed as a "phase" or "cute."

Please, please don't treat childlike faith with suspicion.

What if instead of questioning whether it's real, we nurtured it? Encouraged it? What if we discipled those kids like we believe their spiritual lives are just as important—if not more—than the adults in our churches?

Children's ministry isn't about giving kids something to do while the grown-ups have church. It is church. They are the Church. Right now.

4. Parents, This Starts At Home

Parents, hear me on this. Teaching your kids to fear the Lord isn't something you can outsource—not even to the best KidMin leader in the world. The church can (and should!) partner with you. But God has given you the front-row seat to your child's heart.

That means discipleship has to happen beyond Sunday.

Are you praying with your kids? Reading the Bible together? Modeling repentance, faith, and humility? Your kids are watching—and your example may teach them more than any lesson ever will.

Let's be honest: we get fired up about sports, school, and success. But are we fired up about helping our kids know and love Jesus?

Don't wait for the "perfect time" to start. Start messy. Start small. Start tonight.

5. Leaders, This Is Holy Ground

Children's ministry leaders—you are not running a program. You are not filling a slot on Sunday morning. You are not just prepping crafts or leading songs. You are standing on holy ground every single time you teach a child about Jesus.

You are shaping the future of the Church. You are watering seeds of truth that may not bloom for years—but when they do, they'll bear fruit that lasts for eternity.

That kid who can't sit still today may be the one who preaches the gospel to nations tomorrow.

That quiet girl who never speaks up in your small group? She might lead worship for thousands someday—or raise a family that changes their community for Christ.

You don't always see the fruit right away. That's okay. You're sowing in faith, not results. Keep sowing.

6. Expect God To Work In Kids' Lives

Finally, let's raise our expectations.

Spurgeon said that even those who believe kids can be saved often don't expect it. Let's change that. Let's pray with expectation. Let's prepare messages, small group lessons, and altar moments with the full faith that God is moving—even in preschoolers.

And let's make sure we include every child in that expectation—including those with special needs.

Just because a child communicates differently, processes things at a different pace, or struggles with behaviors that don't fit our typical classroom mold—does not mean the Spirit of God can't move in their heart. In fact, some of the purest, most heartfelt expressions of faith I've ever seen have come from children with special needs.

God sees them. God loves them. And God can work powerfully in and through them.

Let's stop acting surprised when a six-year-old loves Jesus.

Let's disciple children—all children—like they already belong to Him.

Because when we do, we align ourselves with what the Spirit is already doing.

~ 15 ~

KING DAVID'S TWO ENCOURAGEMENTS TO PARENTS AND TEACHERS

The first is the encouragement of godly example. David said, "Come, children, listen to me: I will teach you to respect and honor the Lord." You're not embarrassed to follow in David's footsteps, are you? Surely you won't hesitate to follow the example of someone who was not only deeply spiritual but also greatly respected. Would you be too proud to walk in the path of the shepherd boy, the giant-slayer, the sweet songwriter of Israel, and the powerful king? Of course not! I believe you'd be thrilled to be like David. But if you're looking for an even higher example than David, listen to the Son of David as He gently says, "Let the little children come to Me, and don't stop them, for the Kingdom of Heaven belongs to such as these." I truly believe these examples will encourage you. You who teach children are not involved in something unimportant; even if someone says, "You're just a Sunday school teacher," the truth is you're taking on a noble role, holding a respected position, and walking in the footsteps of some remarkable people.

We love to see people with influence and leadership in society take an interest in Sunday schools. One major weakness in many churches is that children are left mainly in the care of younger people, while older members—who have more wisdom—often pay them little attention. And sadly, wealthy members sometimes step back, acting as though teaching poor children isn't their responsibility—when it absolutely is. I'm hoping for the day when strong leaders in the church will stand up and take part in this battle against spiritual darkness. In the United States, we've heard of presidents, judges, members of Congress, and others in high positions—not "lowering themselves" (I dislike that phrase)—but honoring themselves by teaching young children in Sunday school. Anyone who teaches a class in Sunday school has earned real respect. I would rather be called "S.S.T." (Sunday School Teacher) than M.A., B.A., or any other title handed out by universities. So please be encouraged, knowing that your work is so meaningful. Let David's royal example, and even more, Christ's divine example, fill you with renewed energy and passion, with confidence and determination to continue in your calling, just as David once said: "Come, children, listen to me: I will teach you to respect the Lord."

The second encouragement is the hope of great success. David said, "Come, children, listen to me," and he didn't say, "Maybe I'll teach you the fear of the Lord," but rather, "I will teach you." He had confidence in the outcome. And even if he hadn't seen the results, others certainly have. The success of Sunday schools! If I were to talk about that, I'd never run out of material—so I'll resist the urge to begin. Many books could be written on the topic, and even then, we might say, "I suppose the world itself couldn't hold all the stories we could tell." In heaven, where the stars eternally praise God and the white-robed crowd throws their crowns at

His feet, we'll witness the success of Sunday schools. And here on earth, where countless children gather each week to sing,

"Gentle Jesus, meek and mild," we already see the results of Sunday school ministry. In nearly every pulpit in our land, in the pews where deacons sit, and among faithful members in worship—you'll find the fruit of Sunday schools. And even far across the ocean, in the islands of the South, in places where people once bowed to idols of wood and stone, you'll find missionaries who first came to Christ through Sunday school—and now their work has reached thousands. All of this adds to the vast and almost unmeasurable impact of Sunday school teaching.

Keep going with your sacred work. Much has been done, but much more remains. Let every past victory stir your heart with new passion. Let the memory of your earlier wins, and every trophy gained for Christ in past battles, fuel your determination to keep moving forward with the responsibilities of today—and the opportunities of tomorrow.

Reflections from Ryan

The Power of Example and Endurance in KidMin

If there's one thing I've learned in all my years of children's ministry, it's this: kids are always watching. They watch how we talk to them, how we pray, how we respond when things don't go our way, how we treat our spouse, how we react when someone cuts us off in traffic on the way to church. They soak in our example more than our words. And that's exactly where Spurgeon starts in this chapter—with David's powerful example.

1. Kids Learn by Watching Your Life

David didn't just say, "Hey kids, go fear the Lord." He said, "Come, children, listen to me; I will teach you the fear of the Lord." Do you notice the posture of that invitation? Come with me. Walk with me. Learn from my life. That's what kids need today.

Whether you're a school teacher, a parent, a grandparent, a small group leader, or a pastor, your greatest influence isn't in your lesson plans or Instagram devotionals—it's in your daily life. You don't have to be perfect (and thank the Lord for that!), but you do have to be real. Kids don't need a superhero. They need a genuine example of someone who loves Jesus, even in the messy moments.

2. You Don't Have to Be Perfect—Just Present

Let me speak especially to those of you who serve in children's ministry each week. You may sometimes feel like what you're doing doesn't matter that much. Maybe no one sees how early you come in to set up chairs or how late you stay to clean up glitter from the craft table. Maybe the fifth grader in your class rolls their eyes during the Bible story. Maybe your own heart is weary because you've been serving for years and you're not sure anyone notices.

But friend—Spurgeon would look you in the eyes and say, "Take heart." And I say the same to you: Don't you dare give up.

You are part of a long and noble line of Christ-followers who have taken the hand of a child and said, "Let me show you what it means to follow Jesus." You stand shoulder to shoulder with King David. With Paul. With Timothy's grandmother Lois. With thousands of faithful, unsung heroes who taught memory verses to squirmy kids, prayed over runny noses, and quietly modeled the faith in homes and church classrooms.

3. Your Faithfulness is More Powerful Than You Know

Spurgeon goes on to say that we should be encouraged not just because of our godly examples, but also because of the immense impact of our work. He reminds us that success in children's ministry isn't measured only in what we see today—but in what God is doing over time.

Sometimes that fruit shows up early. Maybe you've had a child come back years later and say, "You taught me when I was in second grade. You helped me fall in love with Jesus." Those moments are precious. But other times, we won't see the harvest until heaven.

That's why Spurgeon's words matter so much. He saw something in David's confident statement: "I will teach you the fear of the Lord." That wasn't arrogance—it was assurance. David knew that if he lived it, spoke it, and invited children into it, something eternal would take root.

Today, you and I can hold on to that same confidence. God has always used ordinary people to do extraordinary things in the lives of children. Think about it: David was a shepherd. Miriam, as a young girl, watched over her baby brother Moses and played a key role in God's plan. Andrew wasn't a famous leader—he simply brought a boy with five loaves and two fish to Jesus, and a miracle followed. And most children's ministry leaders I know aren't looking for applause—they just love kids and love Jesus.

4. You're Shaping Kingdom Leaders

Let me encourage you with this: you don't need to be the flashiest communicator, the trendiest social media influencer, or the best game planner. You need to be faithful. You need to keep showing up, praying hard, loving well, and planting seeds. Because those seeds grow into something more than we can imagine.

Think about the scope of what Spurgeon describes—pulpits filled with former Sunday school kids, missionaries changing lives across oceans, and children who once sang "Gentle Jesus, meek and mild" growing into bold Kingdom leaders. This isn't fairy tale talk. It's reality.

Right now, in your ministry, you are shaping tomorrow's missionaries, pastors, parents, youth leaders, and teachers. And even more than that—you're raising up disciples of Jesus who will live for Him in workplaces, schools, and neighborhoods.

So let me ask you:

- Are you discouraged? Remember, your example matters more than you think.
- Are you feeling invisible? God sees every act of faithfulness you offer.
- Are you weary? Ask the Lord for renewed strength and vision. He gives it.
- Are you wondering if your kids are even getting it? Trust the Word you've planted. It never returns void.

5. The Church and Home Together Can Change the World

And if you're a parent reading this—please hear me: you are your child's number one teacher. Church matters. Sunday school matters. But none of them can replace the example you set at home. Your kids see how you pray (or don't). They hear how you talk about others. They pick up on your attitude toward church. They know if Jesus is just something you do on Sundays or someone you live for every day.

But here's the hope: You don't have to do this alone. We're in this together—parents, teachers, volunteers, pastors. The church and the home working together can change the world, one child at a time.

So let's take Spurgeon's words to heart. Let's model the fear of the Lord. Let's keep teaching, even when we don't see immediate results. Let's celebrate every small victory, every answered prayer, every "aha" moment in a child's eyes. Let's press on, confident that our labor is not in vain.

Because one day, in heaven, we're going to meet the kids we taught—and their kids, and their grandkids. And we'll say, "It was worth it."

Keep planting. Keep praying. Keep walking with Jesus. The Kingdom belongs to such as these.

~ 16 ~

CHILDHOOD AND HOLY SCRIPTURE

Paul taught young Timothy the gospel personally: he not only made him hear his teaching, but also see it lived out. We can't force truth into people, but we can make our teaching clear and firm, and make sure our lives back it up. Truth and holiness are the most powerful weapons against lies and ungodliness. The apostle said to Timothy, "Keep holding on to the things you've learned and been convinced of, knowing who taught them to you."

He then pointed to another powerful influence that had deeply helped the young preacher—namely, Timothy's early knowledge of the Holy Scriptures. This was one of the strongest foundations in Timothy's life. His early training acted like an anchor, keeping him steady and grounded in a world drifting off course. What a blessing, that the apostle could say of him, "From childhood you have known the Holy Scriptures, which are able to make you wise for salvation through faith in Christ Jesus!"

To prepare for what lies ahead, we only need to do three things: preach the gospel, live the gospel, and teach children God's Word. That last one deserves special attention, because God still uses the praises and words of little children to silence the enemy.

It's foolish to think that human wisdom is the answer to human wisdom, or that Satan can defeat Satan. Not at all. Just as Moses lifted up the bronze snake in the desert when fiery serpents were biting the people, we must lift up the cross of Christ. People will look and live. Bring the children, hold them up, and help them fix their eyes on the remedy God has provided—because there's still life in a look. There's still healing from the deadly poison of sin in the name of Jesus. There's still no cure for midnight but the rising sun; no hope for a dark world except the light that shines on everyone. Shine, O Sun of Righteousness—shine and scatter the fog, the clouds, and the darkness. Stick to the apostles' strategy, and you can trust you'll see apostles' results. Preach Christ. Preach the Word, whether it's convenient or not. And teach the children. One of God's key ways of keeping weeds out of His fields is to plant good seed early.

God's grace started working in Timothy through early instruction—"From childhood you have known the Holy Scriptures."

Look at the timing of that instruction. The phrase "from childhood" is more accurately "from infancy," or as the updated translation says, "from a baby." It doesn't mean a child old enough to read or reason, but a little one just barely out of the cradle. From babyhood, Timothy had been introduced to the sacred writings. This is clearly meant to show that we can't start too early when it comes to teaching our children the Bible. Babies begin learning long before we realize it. In the first months of life, a child learns more than we think. They quickly learn their mother's love and their own dependence. And if the mother is wise, the child also begins to understand the meaning of obedience and submitting their will to someone higher. That could become the theme of their whole life. If a child learns obedience early, it can prevent countless tears—for both child and mother. There's a real loss when even babyhood is left untouched.

Children can start learning the Scriptures as soon as they're able to understand anything. It's remarkable—something I've heard many teachers say—that kids often learn to read better from the Bible than from any other book. I'm not sure why—maybe it's the straightforward language—but I believe it's true. A Bible story will often stick when a history lesson is forgotten. The Bible is suited to human hearts of every age, which makes it especially suited to children. It's a mistake to think we need to start with something else and then "build up" to Scripture. The Bible is the perfect book for the start of life. Sure, parts of it are too deep for a child—just as they're too deep for any of us. There are oceans where great creatures can swim, but there are also shallow brooks where a lamb can splash. Wise teachers know how to guide little ones to green pastures and still waters.

I was struck, while reading the biography of that great servant of God whom many of us still miss deeply—the Earl of Shaftesbury—that his first spiritual impressions came through a humble woman. The faith that shaped him—Shaftesbury, the man of God and friend of the needy—was first planted in the nursery. Young Lord Ashley had a godly nurse who told him about the things of God. He shared that she died before he turned seven—clear proof that, even at that early age, his heart had been touched by the Spirit of God, through the faithful influence of an ordinary caregiver. Blessed among women was she—whose name we don't even know—but who left an eternal impact by teaching that chosen child. Let every young nanny, babysitter, or caregiver take note.

Give us the first seven years of a child's life—with God's help—and we can stand strong against the world, the flesh, and the devil. Those early years, while the clay is still soft, go a long way toward shaping the final form. Don't ever think that teaching children is any less important than preaching to adults. On the contrary—you get them first, and the first impressions often last the longest. May they be good and godly ones! As people near the end of their lives, the memories that come flooding back are most often the ones formed when they were sitting on their mother's lap. That's what made Dr. Guthrie ask for a "children's hymn" on his deathbed—it was a natural instinct to return to those earliest memories and close the loop of life. The things of childhood are often the sweetest in old age. As we grow older, we start to peel away some of life's clutter and get back to our truest selves. That's why the old songs rise to our lips, and the old lessons return to our minds. Childhood teachings leave deep and lasting marks—let's make sure those marks are pointing our children to God.

Now, notice how wisely Timothy's teachers were chosen. We don't have to guess who taught young Timothy. In the first chapter of this same letter, Paul says, "I'm reminded of your sincere faith, which first lived in your grandmother Lois and in your mother Eunice, and I'm convinced now lives in you also." Grandmother Lois and mother Eunice both had a hand in his spiritual training. Who better to teach children than their own family? Timothy's father was a Greek—most likely a non-believer—but the boy was blessed with a godly grandmother (who's often a child's most beloved relative), and a devoted mother. She had once been a faithful Jew and later became a strong Christian. It was her daily joy to teach her child the Word of God. Mothers, you have a sacred responsibility from the Lord! God has essentially said to you, "Take care of this child for Me, and I will reward you." You're preparing a future man of God so he can be equipped for every good work.

And if God grants you a long life, you may one day hear that same little boy preaching to crowds. And in your heart, you'll know that the quiet lessons taught in the nursery helped lead him to love and serve God.

To those who think that a mother staying home with her young children isn't doing "ministry"—nothing could be further from the truth. That godly mother may not always be able to leave home and attend church events, but don't think she's absent from the church's mission. On the contrary, she's doing the Lord's most important work. Mothers, raising your children in the Lord is your highest and most urgent calling. Christian women, when you teach your children the Holy Scriptures, you are serving God just as much as Moses when he led Israel, or Solomon when he built the temple.

Reflections from Ryan

The One Foundation That Will Never Shake

There's something deeply encouraging—and deeply convicting—about Charles Spurgeon's focus on teaching the Scriptures to children from the earliest age. As I reflect on his words, I can't help but think about the incredible opportunity and responsibility we have as ministry leaders and parents in this generation. The need to plant the Word of God into young hearts has never been greater. We are raising kids in a world full of confusion, compromise, and distraction, and the Bible remains the one foundation that will never shake.

Spurgeon's reminder that Timothy "from infancy" knew the Holy Scriptures is a wake-up call. In a culture where people are always waiting for the "right time" to teach their kids spiritual truths—maybe when they're older, when they can read, when they can sit still—Spurgeon shouts across time, Start now! Start while their hearts are soft. Start while they're asking questions. Start when they're still sitting in your lap and climbing into your bed at night. There's no such thing as "too early" when it comes to planting God's Word.

I talk to ministry leaders every day who are tired. You're pulled in a dozen directions. You're managing volunteers, prepping lessons, answering parent emails, and trying to keep a smile on your face. It's easy to get so busy doing "children's ministry" that we forget what the ministry is all about—bringing children to Jesus by helping them know, love, and live the Word of God.

Let me share a few thoughts that I believe can help us live out the spirit of this chapter in practical ways.

1. Scripture Is Still The Best Curriculum

You can have the coolest kids' space, the slickest graphics, and the most entertaining worship set—but if the Word of God isn't central to your teaching, you're building on sand. Today's kids don't need more noise or flash. They need truth. The Bible has a way of cutting through everything else and speaking directly to the heart.

Sometimes we overcomplicate our curriculum. We think we have to reinvent the wheel. But the truth is, the same Scriptures that shaped Timothy can shape the kids in your ministry today. Don't be afraid to teach the Bible plainly and clearly. Don't be afraid to challenge your kids with deep truths. They can handle more than we give them credit for.

2. Parents Are The Primary Disciplers—We're The Support Crew

One of my biggest takeaways from this chapter is the emphasis Spurgeon places on Timothy's mother and grandmother. Lois and Eunice weren't seminary grads. They didn't have KidMin budgets or Instagram accounts. They were faithful women who opened the Word of God with a child they loved.

Children's pastors and leaders, let's be clear: we are not called to replace the spiritual influence of the home—we are called to reinforce it. One hour a week in a classroom can't compete with the impact of a mom or dad who prays with their child, reads Scripture, and models obedience.

Let's do everything we can to equip parents. Give them simple take-home tools. Encourage them. Remind them that they are their child's most important spiritual leader. Many parents feel unqualified. They think, "I didn't grow up with this," or "I don't know enough." Encourage them anyway. Remind them that God often uses ordinary people to do extraordinary things—just like He used a nurse in the life of Lord Shaftesbury, as Spurgeon mentioned.

3. Begin Earlier Than You Think

When Spurgeon talks about teaching children the Scriptures "from a babe," it reminds me how important those early years are. If you lead in a church that has a nursery or early childhood ministry, please don't overlook it. Your crib and toddler volunteers are doing sacred work. What a gift to begin shaping little hearts while they are still learning to speak and walk!

If you're a parent of little ones, don't underestimate the power of spiritual routines. Pray before meals. Speak Scripture over them while you rock them to sleep. Let them see your Bible open. These quiet moments plant seeds that may not sprout for years, but they will take root.

4. God's Word Is Not Too Big For Kids

Spurgeon points out something that we often forget: the Bible is written for people of all ages. Yes, some parts are deep. But there are also streams of living water where the youngest children can safely wade. I've found that kids often understand and remember Bible truths even better than adults do, because they don't come with as much skepticism or baggage.

Teach your kids real Scripture—not just summaries. Let them hear the actual words of Jesus. Help them memorize verses. Let them wrestle with stories. One of the best things you can do is create a culture in your ministry where the Bible is opened, read, and honored every single week.

5. Your Role In Children's Ministry Is Eternal

Every time you show up to teach a class, run a game, or lead a song, you are helping prepare the next generation of Jesus-followers. There's no such thing as a "small" role when it comes to ministering to kids.

God may very well be raising up the next thought-leader, evangelist, or world-changer in your Sunday school room or VBS program. Even more important—He may be raising up a faithful man or woman of God who will live out their faith as a nurse, teacher, parent, or missionary. You may not always see the fruit, but you are sowing seeds that will last for eternity.

6. Impressions Made In Childhood Last A Lifetime

As someone who's now in my 50s, I can say with full confidence: the things I remember most clearly about my faith didn't happen in adulthood—they happened in childhood. I remember my parents praying with me. I remember those sock puppets in Sunday school. I remember memorizing verses with my church friends. Those things shape your soul.

That's why we must never minimize what's happening right now in children's ministry. The songs you sing, the Bible stories you tell, the love you show—all of it creates spiritual anchors that kids will carry with them into college, into marriage, and into the final moments of life.

Final Thoughts

Let's be bold in teaching children the Word of God. Let's be urgent, not waiting until "they're ready," but beginning the moment they're born. Let's link arms with parents and caregivers and cheer them on in this holy calling. And above all, let's never forget that when we teach children Scripture, we are doing the very work of God. As Spurgeon reminds us, "One of God's chief methods for preserving His fields from tares, is to sow them early with wheat."

Let's keep planting. The harvest will come.

~ 17 ~

WITNESSES FOR GOD CONVERTED IN YOUTH

I get the feeling that Elijah didn't think too highly of Obadiah. He doesn't treat him with much respect, and actually speaks to him more sharply than you'd expect between two fellow believers. Elijah was a man of bold action—always out front, nothing to hide. Obadiah, on the other hand, was a quiet believer—genuine and faithful, but in a really tough spot, and so he had to do his duty in a more discreet way. His faith in the Lord shaped how he lived, but it didn't push him to leave the king's court.

Even after this conversation, Elijah seems to act like Obadiah and those like him didn't matter much. He says, "They've torn down Your altars and killed Your prophets with the sword, and I—only I—am left, and they're trying to kill me too." But Elijah knew full well that Obadiah was still around. Obadiah may not have been a prophet, but he was still a man of significance. Yet Elijah pretty much overlooks him, as if he didn't count in the bigger battle. Maybe it's because Elijah, this iron-willed prophet of fire and thunder, didn't put much stock in anyone who wasn't on the front lines like he was.

This kind of thinking is common. People who are passionate and bold often underestimate the quiet, faithful believers working behind the scenes. These unseen servants of God might be doing their best under hard circumstances, facing intense opposition, and avoiding any spotlight—but they still matter. However, those who live out their faith in the public eye can sometimes fail to recognize them. These behind-the-scenes "stars" get lost in the glow of someone God raises up to shine like a blazing sun in the darkness. Elijah tore through Israel like a lightning bolt from Heaven, so naturally he'd be a little impatient with those who were slower or less flashy. In some ways, it's like the dynamic between Martha and Mary all over again.

God doesn't like it when His most prominent servants look down on their quieter coworkers. I think that's why He arranged it so that Obadiah became necessary to Elijah when it was time to face the angry king. God told Elijah to go present himself to Ahab, and he obeys. But first, he approaches the palace manager—Obadiah—to break the news to the king and help prepare him. Ahab was already furious because of the long drought, and might lash out and kill Elijah on the spot. This approach gave Ahab some time to cool off before meeting the prophet.

So Elijah has a conversation with Obadiah and tells him to go say to Ahab, "Elijah is here." Sometimes the straightest path to our goal means taking a bit of a detour. It's interesting that Obadiah—someone much less bold—is used in this way to help a man of Elijah's stature. Elijah, who never feared kings, still ends up needing a more cautious man's help.

This story shows us something important: God will never leave Himself without witnesses in this world. And not only that— He makes sure there are witnesses even in the darkest places. Imagine what it must've been like to be a true believer living in Ahab's royal court! Even if Jezebel were the only sinner there, she would've made it bad enough. That proud, strong-willed queen from Sidon completely controlled weak Ahab. He might never have become such a persecutor if she hadn't pushed him to it. Jezebel hated the worship of Jehovah and looked down on the simple faith of Israel compared to the showy religion of Sidon. And Ahab had to give in to her every demand. She didn't tolerate opposition and was ruthless when provoked.

Yet even in that toxic royal court, Obadiah—who was in charge of the palace—was a man who deeply feared God. Never be shocked to find a believer in the most unlikely places. God's grace can survive where you'd never expect it to last an hour.

Joseph feared God in Pharaoh's court. Daniel served as a trusted advisor to Nebuchadnezzar. Mordecai stood at the gate of King Ahasuerus. Pilate's wife pleaded for Jesus' life. And there were believers even in Caesar's household. Think about that— finding diamonds in a place as vile as Nero's palace! These Roman believers weren't just Christians; they were examples of love and generosity for all other believers. There's not a single place in this country so dark that it doesn't have at least some light. Even the deepest caves of sin still hold a flicker of hope. Don't be afraid— you may find followers of Jesus even in what feels like the devil's backyard. In Ahab's palace, you'll meet an Obadiah who's thrilled to hang out with the persecuted saints and leaves royal court life to help hide God's prophets.

One more thing I've noticed: many of God's strongest wit- nesses are people who were converted when they were young. God seems to take joy in using these individuals as His flag-bear- ers in difficult times. Think of Samuel! When all of Israel was fed up with the wickedness of Eli's sons, it was young Samuel who served in the Lord's presence. Look at David! Even as a shepherd boy, he filled the lonely hills with songs of praise and music from his harp. And Josiah! When the nation had turned its back on God, it was a child—Josiah—who tore down Baal's altars and burned the bones of its priests. Daniel was just a teen when he chose purity and obedience to God.

Even now, the Lord is raising up the next generation. Maybe there's a young Luther sitting on his mom's lap, a future Calvin learning in Sunday school, or a little Zwingle singing songs to Jesus. Sure, this world might get worse—I sometimes think it will, based on what we see—but the Lord is preparing for that. The days look dark and threatening, and maybe the evening will fade into a night darker than we've ever known. But God's work is safe in His hands. It won't stall because of a shortage of workers. Don't reach out like Uzzah did to steady the ark—God will carry His work forward on His terms. Christ will not fail or be discouraged. God may bury His workers, but His work continues.

Even if there's no godly king in the palace, God will place a faithful palace official who fears the Lord from his youth and is ready to protect His prophets until better days come. So take heart. Look forward with hope. Nothing truly valuable is in danger while God sits on the throne. His reinforcements are already on the way—and their drums beat with victory.

Reflections from Ryan

Living as Obadiahs in Ahab's World

One of the most powerful truths from this chapter is that God has always had His people—especially young people—set apart for His purposes. Whether it's a bold Elijah standing on the mountaintop or a quiet Obadiah faithfully serving behind the scenes, the Lord never leaves Himself without a witness. And you know what? That truth is just as real today in your church, your school, and yes, even in your living room.

Obadiah isn't the loudest name in Scripture, but wow, what a legacy. In the middle of one of the darkest, most idolatrous environments in all of Israel's history—Ahab and Jezebel's royal court—he didn't just survive; he thrived. He feared the Lord greatly from his youth and ended up protecting a hundred of God's prophets during a nationwide spiritual crisis. How many of us can say we've had that kind of courage when the pressure's on?

And yet, isn't it easy to feel like we don't measure up unless we're more like Elijah—front and center, fire from heaven, challenging the king? The reality is that most of us, whether we're teaching children's church, parenting a toddler, or directing a children's ministry, feel more like Obadiah. We're not on the conference stage. We're not trending on social media. We're just faithfully doing what God has asked us to do— even if no one claps.

But Spurgeon helps us see that God doesn't need only Elijahs. He uses Obadiahs, too. And in fact, He delights in using those who have feared Him since their youth. That's where this truth lands so heavily for me as a children's ministry leader and as a dad. What we do with kids matters. The investment we make in their young hearts could be the very thing that sustains the church in the next generation.

We often talk about raising up leaders—but do we realize that today's wide-eyed third grader might be tomorrow's "Obadiah," sent into a hostile world not just to survive, but to protect the flame of truth when everything else seems dark?

1. Quiet Faith Still Counts

Let's be honest—there's a kind of temptation in ministry to measure impact by visibility. "If I had more kids in my ministry…" "If my volunteers were more committed…" "If I just had more budget or more time or more support from leadership…" And before we know it, we're thinking like Elijah—"I'm the only one left!" But God's story reminds us: You are not the only one. You're not alone. There are quiet, faithful believers like Obadiah in cubicles, classrooms, kitchens, and coffee shops all over your community. And maybe some of them are sitting on the rug in your kids' church right now, listening to a lesson on David and Goliath or coloring a memory verse.

They might not have Elijah's voice. They might not want to stand on a stage. But they're growing. Watching. Learning. And in time, God will use them in ways you never saw coming.

As leaders and parents, let's be the kind of people who notice the Obadiahs. Let's not overlook the shy kid in the back row, the volunteer who always shows up but never speaks up, or the young man or woman who's still figuring out where they fit in the kingdom. God has big plans for them. He always has.

2. Youth Is No Barrier To Boldness

Spurgeon walks us through example after example of young people who changed history: Samuel, David, Josiah, Daniel. They weren't "just kids." They were God's kids. And they were ready when He called.

Do you believe the same could be true of the kids in your life?

I once heard someone say, "Don't underestimate what God can do in the heart of a child." That's not just a cute quote—it's a challenge. We aren't just entertaining kids on Sundays. We are discipling them. Raising warriors. Cultivating world changers.

This means we have to take seriously the responsibility of planting seeds of truth, nurturing faith, and pointing them constantly to Jesus. Because when the drought comes—when the culture around them grows darker—they will need deep roots.

Your faithfulness today might be why a child remains faithful twenty years from now in a secular workplace or an antagonistic environment. Your investment might be the reason a child chooses purity. Or a young person says yes to God's call to preach. Or why a teenager stands up for truth in a world that calls truth hate.

You may never see the full impact of your work—but rest assured, God does.

3. God Is Never Caught Off Guard

This chapter ends with such a comforting reminder: the Lord isn't pacing heaven wondering how He's going to keep His church alive. He's already preparing the next generation. In fact, some of His greatest warriors are still learning to read, still sitting in booster seats, still memorizing the books of the Bible.

They're in your classroom. They're in your kitchen. They're on your Wednesday night van route. Some of them don't know the Lord yet—but they will. Others are already asking questions that reveal a tender heart God is shaping. Some will be Elijahs, and some will be Obadiahs. But all will be part of God's plan.

So here's my challenge to you:

Don't minimize the importance of what you do week after week with kids.

Don't assume your quiet faithfulness doesn't matter.

Don't give up when it feels like the world is getting darker.

And don't forget—God has witnesses everywhere, even in places that feel hopeless.

Let's raise up Obadiahs. Let's train up Esthers. Let's disciple Daniels. Let's tell the stories of brave faith and remind our kids that the same God who worked through those young people in the Bible wants to work through them today.

Keep showing up. Keep planting seeds. Keep praying over those kids' names.

Because while the world may be looking for the next Elijah, God is also calling a generation of Obadiahs—young hearts who will grow up to protect His truth in unlikely places.

And maybe, just maybe, you're the one He's using to help them get there.

~ 18 ~

OBADIAH'S EARLY FAITH

Obadiah had faith from a young age—"I, your servant, have feared the Lord since my youth." Oh, how I pray that every young person growing up into adulthood would be able to say the same! What a blessing it is for people to have this kind of testimony!

We're not told exactly how Obadiah came to fear the Lord so early in life. The person who introduced him to faith in Jehovah isn't named. Still, it's reasonable to assume that he had godly parents. The clue may lie in his name. It's not a stretch to think that his mother or father gave him the name "Obadiah," which means "servant of the Lord," as a reflection of their own faith. Back in those days, when believers were being persecuted, and the name of Jehovah was mocked because of the widespread worship of idols like the calves of Bethel and the images of Baal, it's unlikely that unbelieving parents would choose a name that honored the Lord. They wouldn't have risked drawing attention or ridicule from their idolatrous neighbors or from those in power. Back when names actually carried meaning, they might've called him "child of Baal" or "servant of Chemosh" if they didn't revere the Lord. Giving him the name "Obadiah" tells me that they sincerely hoped their son would serve Jehovah and never bow down to the disgusting idols promoted by the Sidonian queen. Whether or not this guess is correct, it remains true that many of the wisest and strongest believers first began to follow God because of the influence of their home environment.

A lot of us could have easily been named "Obadiah" ourselves—we were raised in homes where our parents introduced us to God before we even understood who He was. Our parents dedicated us to God as infants. Many tears of prayer were shed over our cribs. We were surrounded by a prayerful, faith-filled atmosphere. Nearly every day we were urged to serve the Lord, and we were lovingly encouraged from a young age to seek Jesus and give Him our hearts.

But even if Obadiah didn't have godly parents, I don't know how else he would have come to know the Lord during such dark times, unless he encountered a kindhearted teacher, a faithful nanny, or maybe even a godly servant or neighbor—someone brave enough to gather children and tell them about the Lord God of Israel. Perhaps a devoted woman helped him learn the Law of the Lord before the priests of Baal could fill his mind with lies. We don't know who helped young Obadiah come to faith—and that's okay, isn't it? You and I don't need recognition if we're faithfully serving God.

Obadiah's early faith had clear signs of being real. The way he described it is especially powerful: "I, your servant, have feared the Lord since my youth." I can hardly remember hearing children's faith described like that in regular conversation. We usually say, "The sweet child loves Jesus," or, "They're so happy in the Lord." And there's nothing wrong with that language—but notice that the Bible often uses the phrase "the fear of the Lord." Scripture says it is "the beginning of wisdom." David himself said, "Come, children, listen to me: I will teach you the fear of the Lord." Children do experience great joy through faith in Jesus, but that joy—when it's real—is filled with a respectful awe of God.

I don't need to say much more about the benefits of early faith, so I'll summarize briefly. Coming to faith early in life saves you from so many regrets. That person never has to say, "I still carry the consequences of my youthful sins." Early faith helps you form friendships that will encourage and support you throughout life, and it keeps you from falling into harmful ones. A Christian young man is less likely to fall into the common traps that ruin health and character. He's more likely to marry a Christian woman and walk with her toward Heaven. He'll choose friends who encourage godly character, not those who tempt him toward sin. Don't underestimate how much your future is shaped by the friends you choose early on. Starting out in bad company makes it hard to turn around. But a person who meets Jesus early in life builds habits of holiness instead of becoming enslaved by bad ones. Habits quickly become second nature, and it's difficult to change them once they're set. But habits formed in youth often stay with you into old age. As the old verse says:

> It's easier if we start
> To serve the Lord when young;
> But sinners growing old in sin
> Are deeply trapped and numb.

That's the truth. I've also noticed that people who come to Christ in childhood often grow in their faith faster than those who come later. They don't have to unlearn as much, and they're not burdened with as many painful memories. The scars and wounds that come from serving the devil for years are avoided by those who come to Jesus early, before the world gets its hooks in them.

As for the impact of early faith on others, I can't praise it enough. There's something so moving about seeing a young person full of grace. What you might overlook in an adult, you can't ignore in a child. Faith in a child has a special power to convince: even skeptics pause and take notice. A child's words stay in the heart. A child's prayer can touch where a preacher's sermon might fail. Childlike faith can inspire older people, too. Seeing a child come to Christ often makes adults say, "If they can find the Lord, why can't I?" God uses the faith of little ones to unlock hearts. Where nothing else can break through, the love of a child might do the trick. It's still true today: "Out of the mouths of babes and infants, You have established strength because of Your enemies, to silence the enemy and the avenger."

Reflections from Ryan

Raising Up Obadiahs

Charles Spurgeon paints a powerful picture in this chapter: a young man named Obadiah who feared the Lord from his youth. His life is a reminder that children aren't just the church of tomorrow—they're fully capable of living for Jesus right now. And if there's one thing I've learned in decades of children's ministry, it's this: when a child finds Jesus early, that changes everything.

Let's talk about how this plays out for you and me—whether you're a ministry leader, a pastor, a parent, or all of the above.

1. Early Faith Is Real Faith. Don't Underestimate It.

Obadiah didn't say, "I learned about God when I was young," or "I started going to temple early on." No, he said, "I, your servant, have feared the Lord from my youth." That's not surface-level religion. That's deep-rooted, reverent, lifelong devotion. And it started when he was a kid.

Here's the challenge: sometimes, even in the church, we unintentionally minimize children's spiritual capacity. We say things like, "Oh, they're too young to really understand," or "Let's wait until they're older before we talk about commitment." But that's not the pattern we see in Scripture. God works in young hearts. He always has. Samuel heard God's voice as a boy. David worshiped God in the fields as a teen. Josiah became king at eight and led a revival in his twenties. And here, Obadiah feared the Lord from his youth.

As children's leaders and parents, we need to raise our expectations. Kids can know God. Kids can serve God. Kids can even suffer for God. We shouldn't be lowering the bar for them—we should be lifting it up and helping them reach it.

2. Your Influence Matters—Probably More Than You Know.

Spurgeon makes a good point: we don't know who led Obadiah to faith. Maybe it was his parents. Maybe it was a faithful servant. Maybe it was a neighbor who dared to whisper truths about Jehovah in a land full of idols. But even though the influence is unnamed, it was undeniably effective.

Here's the thing—we're all called to be that unnamed influence. The kids in our ministries may never write our names in their memoirs, but they'll carry our fingerprints for life. The way we teach, the way we model worship, the way we respond to stress, the way we pray—it all sinks in.

Don't ever think you're wasting your time by rocking babies in the nursery, writing silly skits for Sunday morning, or having another bedtime devotional that feels like a mess. You are sowing seeds. You're forming patterns of thinking, speaking, and believing that may last for decades. If Obadiah grew up fearing the Lord, someone had to plant that seed. Be the seed-planter.

3. Kids Need More Than Fun—They Need Awe.

One of the most striking parts of this chapter is the phrase "I fear the Lord." That's a concept we've somewhat lost in modern children's ministry. We're good at excitement. We're good at making kids laugh. We're great at games, music, and motion. And all of that is wonderful. We want ministry to be fun!

But let's not lose the reverence.

Obadiah didn't just say, "I liked going to church" or "I had a great time in kids' church." He said, "I feared the Lord." There was a weight to his faith. A seriousness. A holy awe.

That doesn't mean we throw out the balloons or cancel the Nerf wars. But it does mean we must be intentional about leading kids into quiet moments with God. Teach them to listen. Help them see that God is not only their best friend, but also their King. Let's disciple kids in a way that they walk away not just entertained, but in awe of a holy God.

4. Early Faith Saves Kids From Years Of Heartbreak.

Spurgeon says it well: when someone finds God early, they're spared a thousand regrets. I've seen it firsthand. A kid who starts following Jesus in elementary school is far more likely to make wise choices in middle school, high school, and beyond. They'll form the right friendships. They'll seek the right guidance. They'll fall, yes—but they'll fall forward into the arms of grace.

I've talked to so many adults who tell me, "I wish I had found Jesus earlier." That's why your work with children is so critical. You are helping them avoid the pain of wandering. You're giving them a foundation before the storms come. You're handing them a compass before they start their journey.

Let's keep this in front of us: early faith isn't just a sweet story. It's a strategic rescue mission.

5. Faith In Kids Impacts Everyone Around Them.

I love how Spurgeon describes the influence of a godly child. When kids love Jesus, people notice. Even hardened adults, skeptical neighbors, or cold-hearted relatives can be moved by the prayer of a child. We've all seen it. A kid's worship can break down walls that sermons never could.

This is why I love putting kids in leadership. Let them pray for the class. Let them share their testimonies. Let them invite their friends. Let them worship in their own voice. When a kid boldly follows Jesus, it becomes a billboard for the gospel.

And here's the amazing ripple effect: when one child comes to Christ, it often pulls the whole family in. I can't count the number of parents who came back to church because their child asked them to. Kids can be some of the best missionaries on the planet.

So what do we take away from Obadiah?

We remember that God still calls young hearts.

We commit to nurturing early faith.

We choose to be the faithful voices behind the scenes.

And we keep believing that a child who fears the Lord may be the one who brings revival to their home, their school, or their generation.

Let's keep planting. Let's keep praying. Let's keep calling kids into something deeper than just fun. Let's invite them into the fear of the Lord, because that's where wisdom begins—and that's where world changers like Obadiah are born.

You're doing more than kids' ministry.

You're raising up Obadiahs.

Keep going.

~ 19 ~

OBADIAH AND ELIJAH

Godly character that begins in youth often leads to a lifetime of faithfulness. Obadiah could say, "I, your servant, have feared the Lord since my youth." Time hadn't changed him. No matter how old he was, his faith hadn't faded. We all tend to like new things, and I've seen people abandon truth just for something different. Dying quickly for your faith in martyrdom is one thing—but enduring slow, constant pressure over a lifetime is an even harder test of faithfulness. Staying faithful to God through years of temptation is a powerful testimony. God's grace turning someone like Saul of Tarsus—a man breathing threats against the church—into the Apostle Paul is amazing. But God's grace preserving a believer for ten, twenty, thirty, forty, or fifty years is just as miraculous and deserves even more praise than it usually gets. Obadiah wasn't changed by the passing years—he was the same faithful man in old age as he had been in his youth.

He also didn't cave in to the popular opinions of his time. Being a follower of the Lord was considered backward, outdated, uneducated—a thing of the past. Baal worship was the "progressive" religion of the day. Everyone in the royal court followed the god of Sidon. My lord worshipped Baal, my lady worshipped Baal—because Queen Jezebel worshipped Baal. But Obadiah stood apart and said, "I, your servant, fear the Lord." Blessed is the person who doesn't follow trends, because trends quickly pass. Even if the current trend leans toward evil, the believer's job is to stick with what is right.

Obadiah remained faithful even without access to public worship or spiritual guidance. The priests and Levites had fled to Judah, prophets had been killed or forced into hiding, and there were no services held in Israel to honor the Lord. The temple was far away in Jerusalem, so he had no opportunities to hear encouraging messages or gain strength from other believers. Yet he continued walking with God.

And on top of that, he faced the challenges of his job. Obadiah was the palace administrator. If he had wanted to, he could have pleased Queen Jezebel by worshipping Baal and likely would've gained even more favor. Instead, he remained loyal to the Lord while serving in King Ahab's palace. He must've had to tread carefully, choose his words with precision, and navigate an environment filled with danger. It's no surprise he became cautious, even wary of Elijah, unsure whether the prophet's instructions would put him in harm's way. Obadiah had to be extremely wise—discerning how to protect his conscience without risking his life. That kind of balance requires skill and integrity. He didn't run away from his job or from his faith. If his work had forced him to compromise, I believe he would have done what the priests and Levites did and fled to Judah, where worship of the Lord was still alive. But since he could stay faithful and still do good in his role, he made the brave choice to remain. Sometimes, when there's no hope of success, it's best to retreat—but the real hero is the one who ignores the retreat signal, puts the telescope to his blind eye like Nelson, and continues the fight. Obadiah was that kind of man. He held the fort. While Jezebel was killing off God's prophets, Obadiah stayed close to her and managed to save at least a hundred of them from her cruelty. Even if he did nothing else, that one act made his life worthwhile. I admire his courage and caution, though I wouldn't want to stand in his shoes. His job was like walking a tightrope—like the famous acrobat Blondin. I wouldn't try it, and I wouldn't advise you to either.

Elijah's path was simpler and bolder. The prophet didn't have to win favor—he was called to confront and correct. He could act openly, without having to calculate every word. Elijah was obviously the greater man when the two met. Obadiah bowed down and called him "My lord Elijah," and rightly so—Elijah was his superior. Still, I must be careful not to judge from Elijah's bold position. Obadiah's ability to run Ahab's house—with Jezebel in it—and still earn God's praise as a man who "feared the Lord greatly" is remarkable.

He stayed faithful even after achieving worldly success—which is no small thing. Nothing tests a person more than prosperity. We all hope for success and work toward it, but how many lose their spiritual wealth while gaining earthly wealth? A man who once loved God's people now calls them "unrefined." He used to care about the message, not the building—but now he's obsessed with stained glass, Gothic cathedrals, marble pulpits, fancy robes, and flower arrangements in the church. As he fills his bank account, he empties his convictions. He drifts from truth and principle as he climbs the social ladder. It's disgraceful, and he would've been the first to call it out years ago. There's nothing noble about this kind of compromise—it's shameful. God help us avoid it. Sadly, many people don't. Their faith isn't built on conviction but convenience. Their religion is less about truth and more about social gain. They don't care about honoring God—they're chasing a rich son-in-law or a dinner invite to the estate. I'm not being sarcastic—I speak sincerely, and with sorrow. I hear these things all the time. We live in a time when mediocrity hides under the mask of respectability. God, give us men made of the same steel as John Knox—or if that's too much, at least give us men like Elijah. And if even that seems too intense, then give us more Obadiahs. Truthfully, Obadiahs might be harder to find than Elijahs—but with God, all things are possible.

Obadiah's lifelong devotion made him a man of deep spiritual strength—especially considering who he was and where he served. A godly man in King Ahab's court? That's a miracle of God's grace. His faith ran deep. He may not have expressed it as boldly as Elijah, but that wasn't his calling. Still, his faith was real, and people knew it. Jezebel surely knew it—she probably despised him but couldn't remove him. Ahab had come to rely on him—maybe even found strength from his presence. Perhaps Ahab kept him around just to prove to Jezebel that he still had a will of his own.

However you explain it, it's amazing to find a man like Obadiah in the middle of such a rebellious environment. Just like it's shocking to find a traitor like Judas among the apostles, it's inspiring to find a faithful servant like Obadiah among Ahab's advisors. God's grace must have been working powerfully to keep a fire of faith burning in such a cold and wicked place.

Obadiah's early commitment to God brought him comfort later in life. When he feared Elijah might be putting him in danger, he reminded the prophet of his lifelong faith: "I, your servant, have feared the Lord from my youth." It's like when David said in old age, "O God, You have taught me from my youth; and I still declare Your wondrous works. Now that I'm old and gray, don't abandon me." Looking back on a life spent serving God brings deep peace. You won't rely on your works for salvation—you know there's no merit in them—but you will be grateful. Think about an old servant who's been with his master since youth—no good master would throw him out when he gets old. Or think about a nurse who raised you and then helped raise your kids—would you send her away in her later years? Of course not. If you can, you'll make sure she's cared for. Well, God is far more loving than we are, and He never turns away His faithful servants.

Reflections from Ryan

Holding the Line in a Culture That's Losing Its Mind

When I read about Obadiah, I can't help but think of the thousands of faithful men and women who serve in children's ministry today. You may not have the spotlight. You may not get the applause. You may be working behind the scenes—just like Obadiah. But your faithfulness matters deeply to God.

Obadiah's story is powerful because it proves that you don't have to be the loudest voice to make the biggest difference. He wasn't standing on Mount Carmel calling down fire. He wasn't confronting kings like Elijah. He was managing a palace filled with idolatry and compromise—and still honoring God in quiet, courageous ways.

Sound familiar?

You might not be in a royal court, but you're probably navigating the messy, complicated world of church politics, team drama, tight budgets, and spiritual battles. And if you're raising kids at home, add in sleep deprivation, emotional exhaustion, and the daily pressure of building a God-honoring family in a world that's sprinting in the opposite direction.

Obadiah teaches us that faithfulness is more than fireworks. It's about steadfast obedience over time—even when it's hard. Especially when it's hard.

Let's take three powerful truths from Obadiah's story and get super practical with them.

1. Start Early—And Stay Steady

Obadiah said, "I have feared the Lord from my youth." That's not just a great line—it's a challenge to all of us: to start early and stay steady. One of the greatest gifts you can give your kids, your volunteers, or the children in your ministry is consistency. I'm not talking about perfection. I'm talking about perseverance.

Parents, your kids don't need you to be superheroes. They need you to keep showing up, praying over them, bringing them to church, reading the Bible—even when they roll their eyes. Especially when they roll their eyes.

Children's ministry leaders, your kids don't need the most entertaining programming or cutting-edge tech (though those can be great tools). What they need most is your heart. They need leaders who genuinely love Jesus and walk with Him—who model faith even on the tough days.

Let your legacy be like Obadiah's: "They feared the Lord from their youth—and they never quit."

If you're discouraged today, I want you to remember this: faithfulness is never wasted. God sees it. He honors it. You're planting seeds that will grow long after you're gone.

2. Don't Let The Culture Call The Shots

Obadiah lived in a culture that had gone completely sideways. Baal worship was in fashion, and everyone who was "in the know" had abandoned the God of Israel. Jezebel hated the truth. The prophets were being hunted down. Obadiah could've gone along with it. He could've said, "I don't want to lose my job," or, "This is just how things are now." But he didn't. He stood firm.

Can I be real for a minute?

We are living in a world where people are calling evil good and good evil. Culture is constantly shifting. Morals are up for grabs. Biblical truth is mocked. The temptation to stay quiet or go along with the crowd is stronger than ever.

But as leaders and parents, we cannot let the culture call the shots for our homes, our classrooms, or our ministries. We have to be rooted in God's Word. That means we speak truth in love. We model integrity. We stay kind—but we stay bold.

Obadiah wasn't obnoxious about his faith, but he was unshakable. And that's what our kids need to see in us. Let's raise kids who aren't afraid to go against the flow—because they've watched us do it first.

3. Your Quiet Faithfulness Can Save Lives

This is my favorite part: Obadiah wasn't just quietly surviving in a toxic palace—he was strategically saving lives. He hid 100 prophets in caves, split into two groups, and fed them with bread and water. That's incredible.

You may not feel like a hero. But I promise you—if you're investing in the next generation, you're doing more than you think.

That Sunday when you set your lesson plan aside to comfort a crying child? That conversation with a young mom who was ready to quit? That Sunday where you wondered if anything you said actually landed?

Those moments matter. They are seeds of life. Sometimes ministry feels like cave work—it's hidden, it's quiet, and it costs you something. But don't give up.

Every snack you hand out, every Bible story you tell, every time you welcome a family impacted by special needs—you are rescuing hearts from a world trying to consume them.

Obadiah was doing "palace work," but his heart belonged to the Lord. You may be doing diaper duty, craft prep, or curriculum edits—but you're in the same fight. You are standing between children and a culture that's trying to redefine truth. Keep standing. Keep serving.

Final Thoughts

Some people are called to be Elijah—bold, visible, prophetic. But others are called to be Obadiah—faithful, steady, strategic. The Church needs both.

If you're an Elijah, don't grow proud. If you're an Obadiah, don't grow discouraged. Wherever God has placed you, be faithful there.

Let me close with this encouragement: when you fear the Lord and walk with Him—not for a year or two, but for a lifetime—you will be like Obadiah. Maybe not famous. Maybe not flashy. But effective, faithful, and eternally fruitful.

Stay the course. Keep the faith. Don't underestimate what God can do through your quiet obedience.

You may feel like you're raising kids in a palace ruled by Jezebel—but if God could preserve Obadiah, He can preserve you too.

And the kids you're investing in? You're not just teaching them songs and stories. You're raising up the next Obadiahs... and maybe even the next Elijahs.

~ 20 ~

ABIJAH'S "SOME GOOD THING"

Jeroboam had turned away from the Lord who had placed him on the throne of Israel, and the time had come for his downfall. God, who often brings warning before judgment, sent sickness into Jeroboam's house—his son Abijah became seriously ill. At that point, the parents remembered an old prophet of the Lord and wanted to hear from him what would happen to the child. Fearing that the prophet would speak judgment over the child if he realized it was Jeroboam's family asking, the king told his wife—an Egyptian princess—to disguise herself as a farmer's wife. He hoped this trick would lead the prophet to give a more favorable message. How foolish of the king to think that a prophet who could see the future wouldn't also see through a disguise! Still, the mother was so desperate to know her child's fate that she left his bedside and traveled to Shiloh to meet the prophet. But her disguise was pointless. The prophet, though physically blind, could still "see"—not just through her act but into the future of her family. She came with superstitious hopes of hearing good fortune, but she left brokenhearted, having heard the truth about her sins and her family's coming ruin.

In the heavy judgment that the prophet Ahijah announced to Jeroboam's wife, there was only one bright spot—just one word of comfort. Sadly, I doubt it gave any comfort to the queen. The child was graciously allowed to die, because "in him there was found some good thing toward the Lord, the God of Israel."

Let's take a moment to think about what little we know of this young prince Abijah. His name itself was fitting. Sometimes a good name is given to a bad person, but in this case, the name matched the boy. His name meant "God is my Father." "Ab" means father, and "Jah" is short for Jehovah—so his name declared that Jehovah was his Father. I wouldn't even mention this if his life hadn't made the name true. If you have a strong biblical name, make sure you don't bring it shame.

There was "some good thing" in this child toward the Lord— but what was it? Who can say? The Bible doesn't specify. There's plenty of room for guesswork. Tradition tries to fill in the blanks, but most of those stories are just made up. Our own guesses are probably as accurate as any of them. In fact, the Bible's silence might be teaching us something: any "good thing" toward the Lord is a true sign of grace. Even though we aren't told about the child's faith directly, we know he had it—because without faith, nothing can be truly pleasing to God. He must have been a young believer in Jehovah, the God of Israel. Maybe it was even Abijah himself who asked his mother to go find the prophet. There were plenty of false prophets near the palace; perhaps Jeroboam wouldn't have gone to Shiloh at all if his son hadn't asked him to. The boy must have believed in the invisible, living God who made the heavens and the earth and worshiped Him with childlike faith.

But I wouldn't be surprised if his love for God was more noticeable than his faith. That's often how it is with children. They more naturally talk about loving Jesus than trusting Him—not because they don't have faith, but because love fits their hearts better. A child's heart is wide open, and love is often its most visible fruit. I have no doubt this boy felt early affection for Jehovah and disliked the idols in his father's palace. He may have even been horrified by the worship of a golden calf. Any child with basic understanding would know it's wrong to compare the Almighty God to a farm animal with horns and hooves. Maybe his sensitive spirit was repelled by the rough, immoral priests his father had gathered from the lowest ranks of society. Whatever form it took, this "good thing" in his heart was real—it was directed toward the Lord, the God of Israel.

It wasn't just a fleeting desire or passing emotion—it was something real and lasting. Something solid. Something that could only be described as a genuine work of grace. That's rare. Many children raised to love God will, at some point, feel stirred in their hearts. But that kind of early feeling is like morning dew—it usually disappears quickly. Not so with Abijah. What he had was something that could rightly be called a "good thing"—a spiritual treasure placed in his heart by the Holy Spirit.

We should take notice of this "good thing" in his heart, espe-cially because we don't know how it got there. God clearly saw it, because He always sees even the smallest movement of our hearts toward Him. But how did it get there? The Bible doesn't say—and that silence teaches us something too. We don't always need to know exactly how a child came to faith. It's not always import-ant to pinpoint the moment or place of conversion. Sometimes it's impossible, especially when the change is slow and gradual. Many adults can't describe the details of their own conversion—how much more with children, especially those raised in godly homes who've always known the truth, like the rich young ruler who said he had kept God's commandments from his youth. How did grace reach Abijah's heart? We know this much—it was God who put it there. But through what means?

The boy likely didn't hear faithful teaching from prophets, and he probably wasn't brought to the temple like Samuel was. His mother was an idol-worshiping princess, and his father one of the most wicked men in history—and yet God's grace reached their son. Did God stir up those thoughts in his young mind? Did the boy reflect and conclude for himself that worshiping a golden calf couldn't possibly be right? That's very possible. Or maybe one day he heard a hymn of praise to Jehovah being sung outside the palace by a faithful worshiper. Or maybe he saw something with his own eyes—like the day his father tried to curse the prophet at Bethel and suddenly his right arm withered. Did the boy cry in fear—or maybe even rejoice when the prophet prayed and the arm was restored? That kind of miracle would've been big news in the palace. A royal child would surely hear about something like that.

Or what if the boy had a godly nurse—someone like the servant girl who helped Naaman's wife? What if she carried him in her arms and sang him psalms or told him stories of Joseph and Samuel? Even in corrupt times, God still had faithful followers in Israel, and perhaps one of them was used to reach the boy's heart. We don't know for sure—and we don't need to. If the sun is shining, we don't need to know the exact moment it rose. If we see "some good thing" in a child, that's reason enough to celebrate—even if we don't know how it got there. God always has ways of getting His grace into even the darkest places. He can bring His truth into the heart of Jeroboam's son even while the king bows down to false gods. As Scripture says, "Out of the mouths of babes and infants, You have established strength because of Your enemies." Lord, we don't always see how You move, but we still worship You for the wonderful things You do.

This "good thing" in Abijah's heart had a very specific direction—it was aimed toward the Lord, the God of Israel. Sometimes we see good things in children directed toward their parents—these are worth nurturing. Some children have a natural kindness or high moral standards—these are valuable too. But only those things directed toward God are sure signs of His grace. The Bible talks about "repentance toward God" and "faith in our Lord Jesus Christ." Which direction the heart is pointed matters most. If someone is walking away from God, every step takes them further from Him. But if they're facing toward God, even the smallest steps bring them closer. This boy had "some good thing" in his heart that was turned toward God—and that's the true mark of grace. His faith, love, reverence, and even his thoughts and prayers—all pointed to the true and living God. This is what we long to see in both children and adults: hearts and minds turning toward the Lord.

That "good thing" in the child also made him deeply loved. We know that because the Bible says, "All Israel will mourn for him." He was likely the next in line for the throne, and faithful Israelites were probably hoping for change once he became king. Maybe even people who didn't care much about religion still noticed the boy and had hopes for a better future under his leadership. When Abijah died, he was the only one in his family to receive genuine grief and a proper burial. The rest of Jeroboam's descendants were devoured by wild animals. It's a beautiful thing when a child has so much of God's grace that they're loved by everyone around them. Of course, not every child has the influence of a royal prince, but even in smaller circles, godly children are often admired. There's something incredibly touching about a child who loves Jesus. I rejoice when I see grace in grown men and women—but it brings tears of joy when I see it in children.

There's a special beauty in these young "rosebuds" from the Lord's garden. Their smallness makes them all the more precious. Even unbelievers may not like Christianity, but when they see grace in children, they often respect it. And sometimes, the Holy Spirit uses that to spark a longing for God in their hearts too.

Reflections from Ryan

Finding "Some Good Thing" in Every Child

I love the phrase Charles Spurgeon focuses on in this chapter—"some good thing toward the Lord." It comes from 1 Kings 14:13, where the prophet Ahijah speaks of young Abijah, the son of King Jeroboam. In a dark and rebellious royal household, where idol worship was the norm and true reverence for God was nearly extinguished, this boy shined. Not with fame. Not with grand accomplishments. Not even with a long life. But with a quiet, inner goodness—something good toward the Lord.

If you're a children's ministry leader, a parent, a grandparent, or a volunteer who loves and serves kids, this truth should encourage you deeply. In a world that seems to drift further from God each day, it's easy to feel overwhelmed. But God still sees, notices, and values what's in the heart of a child.

And so should we.

1. God Sees The Heart

In ministry, we often look for visible fruit: attendance numbers, decisions for Christ, raised hands, or volunteers recruited. But God sees beyond all that. He sees what's happening deep inside a child's heart—those quiet thoughts, the whispered prayers, the early stirrings of faith. As Spurgeon reminds us, we don't know how Abijah's heart turned toward God. We just know that it did. And that was enough for God to take notice.

We need to learn from that. Just because a child isn't raising their hands in worship, memorizing verses the fastest, or leading prayer in front of others doesn't mean God isn't doing a real, beautiful work inside them. Our job is to look for the direction of the heart, not just the performance of it.

In your ministry or home, ask God to help you see what He sees. That shy child who listens more than speaks. The fifth grader who always shows kindness. The preschooler who shows compassion for someone hurting. These may not look "spiritual" on the surface, but they might just be signs of "some good thing toward the Lord."

2. We Don't Always Know How Faith Begins In A Child

This part of the story hit me hard. Here's a boy, growing up in a spiritually hostile environment. His dad was one of Israel's worst kings. His mom was a foreign princess, steeped in idol worship. And yet, this child somehow developed a heart for the Lord.

That tells me something important: God is not limited by environment.

I've met leaders who serve in small churches, rural areas, or broken communities and feel like they're failing the next generation because they can't offer everything a bigger church might. I've heard parents worry that they're not spiritual enough, or that their kids will never "get it" because of the chaos at home. But Abijah's story reminds us that God is sovereign. His Spirit can reach any child, in any place, at any time.

Did Abijah have a godly nurse? Did he overhear someone praising Jehovah in the palace courtyard? Did he witness a miracle that marked him for life? We don't know. But we know something sparked that faith.

So don't underestimate the power of a single Bible story, a heartfelt worship song, a simple prayer, or one faithful adult investing in a child. You may never know how deeply those seeds are planted.

3. A Child's Faith May Look Different Than An Adult's

Spurgeon points out that a child's first visible spiritual fruit is often love more than faith. That rings true in my experience. Children often express their relationship with God emotionally: "I love Jesus," "I want to be with Him," or "Jesus is my friend." They may not articulate deep theological truths, but their hearts are often pure and sincere.

Let's not dismiss that. Let's nurture it.

When a child says, "I love Jesus," resist the urge to say, "But do you really understand?" That kind of love—genuine and untangled by cynicism—is exactly what Jesus celebrates. In fact, He told us we should become like little children if we want to enter the kingdom.

As ministry leaders, we must help children develop both love and faith. But let's not rush it. Let's give them space to grow, to question, and to discover Jesus in a way that connects with their hearts first. Theology can come later. What matters most is that the direction of their heart is toward God.

4. Celebrate The Hidden Wins

When Abijah died, all of Israel mourned for him. The nation recognized something special in him—something hopeful. Something pure. Something different from his father and family.

Let's be leaders and parents who notice that "good thing" in kids and call it out.

When you see a child stand up for what's right, celebrate it.

When a child shows compassion, say something.

When a quiet child prays sincerely, affirm it.

You have no idea how your encouragement might shape their view of God and themselves. Let's not just celebrate when kids get baptized or go on missions trips—let's celebrate the daily fruit of a heart pointed toward the Lord.

5. God Uses Children To Spark Revival

Abijah never made it to the throne. But the fact that his short life is recorded in Scripture tells us how seriously God takes the spiritual lives of children.

That's a reminder we need today more than ever.

Children are not the "future Church." They're present-day disciples. When we minister to them, we're not babysitting or entertaining. We're partnering with the Holy Spirit to raise up worshipers, leaders, missionaries, and revival-starters.

And let's not forget: many adults have come to faith by watching the simple faith of a child. God often uses their purity, humility, and passion to convict hearts and stir others to action.

So let's lean into that. Let's create environments in our homes and ministries where kids are free to ask big questions, encounter a big God, and express their faith in big (and small) ways.

Final Thoughts

In Abijah, God found some good thing. And He sees that same potential in the kids you serve each week. Your job is to water those seeds, tend the soil, and trust the Lord of the harvest.

You may not always see the fruit. But take heart—God sees what you can't. And one day, the same God who honored Abijah will honor your faithful investment in His children.

Keep showing up. Keep believing. Keep planting.

There's "some good thing" growing, even now.

~ 21 ~

ABIJAH'S "SOME GOOD THING"—PART 2

He didn't wear religious badges or showy symbols, but he had a gentle and humble spirit. He may not have been much of a talker—otherwise, it might have been said, "He has spoken good things about the God of Israel." He may have been shy, quiet, and almost silent, but the good thing was in him. And this is what we want for all our loved ones—a work of God's grace deep inside. What really matters is not the religious clothing or the spiritual-sounding talk, but having the life of God within us—thinking and feeling as Jesus would because His life is alive in us. Outward religion has little value unless it flows from an inward transformation. True grace isn't something you can just put on and take off like clothes; it becomes a real part of who you are. This child's faith was the real deal—personal, inward, and genuine. May all our children have something truly good within them!

We're told that this good thing "was found" in him, which means it was noticeable without much effort. The word "found" is used even when it doesn't involve a long search. Doesn't the Lord say, "I was found by those who didn't even look for Me"? When a child's faith is sincere, it shows. Children are usually less guarded than adults; they speak freely from the heart. A child's love for

God often shows outwardly, surprising guests with their honest and simple words that reveal their faith. Many people in Tirzah couldn't help but notice this boy had something good toward God. They may not have liked it or may have hoped the bad influences around him would silence it—but still, they saw it. It was obvious.

At the same time, the word "found" has another layer of meaning: it suggests that even when God—who sees and searches every heart—looked into this child's life, He found something worth honoring. God, who can't be fooled, discovered "some good thing" in him. It wasn't fake religion—it was real and precious. May that be true for us as well when our hearts are tested! Maybe his father got angry with him for following God, but whatever trials the boy faced, he came through with his faith intact. There's also a sense of surprise in the phrase. How did this good thing end up in that child? "Some good thing was found in him," like a treasure hidden in a field. A farmer going about his work suddenly uncovers treasure with his plow—he finds it, even though he has no idea how it got there. That's what it was like with this child: despite being in such a difficult environment, everyone was shocked to discover he had something real and good for the Lord. We don't know the details of how God worked in his heart, what it looked like, or what he did—but the evidence was there. It was real grace, right where nobody expected it.

This reminds me of many of the children God calls and saves in the back alleys and housing projects of our big cities. You won't always be able to list out their spiritual experiences or measure every step of their journey. You won't always know the exact moment or method of their conversion. But like Abijah, you simply rejoice to discover this "little miracle of grace" with God's mark on it. The old prophet confirmed the young prince was a true follower of the Lord—and in the same way, God places His seal on children who've been made new by His Spirit. We must be ready to accept that grace, even when it doesn't come with dramatic stories or outward signs. Let's be thankful when we see these works of the Holy Spirit, even if we can't fully explain them.

All we're told is that there was in him "some good thing"— which suggests it was just a beginning, a small spark of grace, the start of spiritual life. Nothing particularly dramatic is said about him; if he had done something heroic for God, it probably would've been recorded. But he was young, without the chance or strength to do great things. Since we're told only that "some good thing" was in him, it means it wasn't a perfect thing or accompanied by all the signs we might hope for. Many good things were missing—but this one good thing was enough. And because of it, God showed him love and spared him from a dishonorable death.

We often miss the "some good thing" in a bad household. The most remarkable part of this story is that a godly child came from Jeroboam's palace. Usually, the mother influences the home, but she was an Egyptian princess and an idol worshiper. The father, Jeroboam, was known for turning Israel away from God. It's amazing to think that he could influence a whole nation to sin but couldn't turn his own child away from God. While his sinful example spread across the land, right there in his own home—right at his feet—was a son completely different from him. Jeroboam's heir had a heart for the Lord.

You wouldn't expect to find faith in a place like that, and you might miss it if you weren't looking closely. Likewise, in the poorest parts of our cities—the alleyways and rundown areas—you might not expect to see God's work. But don't assume He's not there. Don't say, "God's grace couldn't be working in these kids." How do you know? One of those ragged children playing in the dirt might have found Jesus through a street mission or a children's program—and one day, that child may sit beside Christ in glory. That child may be the brightest gem, even if hidden among the rubble. That diamond might be lying on a trash heap—but if that child has "some good thing toward the Lord," then their background doesn't make them less valuable. Maybe their dad is a thief, and their mom drinks too much—but don't look down on them.

There's a story about a pastor in Ireland who saw a ragged little boy standing near the church entrance every Sunday, listening intently to the sermon. The boy always disappeared quickly afterward, and no one could figure out who he was. One Sunday, the pastor preached from the verse, "His own right hand and His holy arm have gotten Him the victory." After that, the boy didn't return. Six weeks later, a man came from the mountains and asked the pastor to visit his dying son. The pastor walked six miles through rough terrain in the rain to get there. As soon as he stepped into the tiny, broken-down hut, the boy—lying in bed—saw him and lifted his hand, shouting, "His own right hand and His holy arm have gotten Him the victory!" That was his final word before dying. Who knows how many kids like that have quietly experienced God's victory, even in the middle of poverty and pain? Let's not ignore the quiet presence of grace just because it shows up in unexpected places.

We don't always understand why God allows His children to suffer. We think, "If that were my child, I would heal them right away." But our Heavenly Father sometimes lets His beloved children go through pain. Jeroboam's godly son was sick—while his wicked father and idol-worshiping mother were not. We might almost wish the opposite. Why should the only godly one in the family be the one to suffer? But God has His purposes. Maybe that suffering child was like a fig that only ripens after being bruised—his sickness helped prepare him for heaven. And perhaps God meant the child's illness to wake up his parents, to turn their hearts toward Him. It drove them to the prophet. Oh, how we wish it had driven them straight to God! Many parents have come to know Jesus through the illness of a child.

But here's something even more amazing—sometimes God's dearest children die young. If it were up to me, I would have said, "Let Jeroboam and his wife die, but let the child live!" Yet it was the child who was taken. Why? Because he was ready. His early death brought glory to God's grace by showing how powerfully it had worked in him. God spared him from the judgment that was coming on his family. While the rest would die by the sword and be eaten by animals, this child died in peace and was buried honorably. His death was actually a proof of God's love and grace.

Some say children who trust Christ shouldn't be welcomed into the church. But if they're ready for heaven, aren't they ready for church too? God, in His kindness, often takes believing children to Himself—not because they lack faith, but because they are so full of it that they're ready. Childlike faith isn't second-class; it's often strong, pure, and ripe for eternity.

reflections from Ryan

You Just May Be Looking At The Next Abijah

Charles Spurgeon's reflections on Abijah—a quiet, God-loving boy in a wicked household—hit close to home for anyone working with kids today. Whether you're a children's ministry leader, a parent, a teacher, or a volunteer, you've likely wondered: Can God really work in this child's life? In this home? In this situation?

Spurgeon's answer is a bold yes—and I believe it's the yes that we need to carry into every classroom, every home, and every conversation with a child. You see, ministry to kids is often not flashy. You may not always see transformation in real time. Some of the best spiritual growth happens quietly, deep in a child's heart—just like with Abijah.

Let's talk about some ways this truth should shape the way we lead and love the kids God has placed in our lives.

1. Stop Looking For Showy Faith—Look For Real Faith

Abijah didn't preach a sermon. He didn't write Psalms. He didn't take a public stand that got recorded in Scripture. What did he do?

He had some good thing in him.

It was quiet. It was personal. It was real.

In children's ministry, we sometimes lean toward measuring impact by what's visible: who memorized the most verses, who sings the loudest during worship, or who answers all the questions. While those things can be signs of growth, they aren't the definition of spiritual health.

Let's not overlook the child who barely speaks but bows his head when we pray. Or the girl who doesn't say much in small group but draws pictures of Jesus every week. Or the boy who holds the door open for others and picks up trash after snack time without being asked. Or the child with special needs who may not communicate like others but shows love through smiles, hugs, or the way they light up during worship.

These "small" things may be glimpses of a big work God is doing on the inside. Let's learn to value genuine over loud.

2. Don't Assume A Bad Home Equals A Hard Heart

Jeroboam's household was a spiritual mess. His wife was an idol worshiper. He was leading an entire nation away from God. Yet in the middle of that darkness—Abijah shines. How?

By God's grace.

This should encourage every ministry leader who's ever worked with a child from a broken home, a non-Christian family, or a spiritually cold environment. You are not wasting your time. God doesn't need ideal circumstances to reach a child's heart.

Sometimes I hear leaders say, "I feel bad for this kid… I wish they had better parents," or "They never bring a Bible," or "Their home life is a mess." I get it. Those things make it harder—but they don't make it impossible.

In fact, some of the strongest Christians I know grew up in spiritually dry homes. Grace can grow in the most unlikely soil. Keep planting. Keep watering. You never know where that "good thing" will be found.

3. Celebrate The Mystery Of A Child's Faith

One of my favorite lines from this chapter is how Spurgeon describes Abijah's faith like a hidden treasure. No one knows exactly how it got there—but it's there.

So often, we try to track every detail of a child's spiritual story: "When did they ask Jesus into their heart?" "What exact words did they pray?" "Do they really understand everything?"

There's nothing wrong with wanting clarity. But let's remember—we're not the Holy Spirit. Salvation isn't a spreadsheet. And sometimes, God works in quiet ways that we only see the fruit of later.

We must trust the Lord to be the One who draws kids to Himself and believe that even a small spark of grace can light a fire in their lives. Don't try to force the story. Just be faithful to disciple and nurture what God is doing.

4. Watch For The "Hidden Gems"

Spurgeon paints a powerful picture of ministry in hard places. He talks about kids in "ragged schools" and slums—those we might overlook because of their surroundings. And then he says: Don't miss the diamonds in the dust.

That's still true today. The child who comes from poverty. The one who struggles with behavior issues. The one who's always in trouble. The one everyone else writes off.

These are the very ones where "some good thing" might be hidden—and it's our privilege to dig for it.

And let's not forget one of the most overlooked groups of all: families impacted by special needs. This is the largest unreached people group in the United States—and one of the most underserved in our churches. Children with special needs often face barriers to inclusion, and their parents often feel isolated, misunderstood, or simply forgotten. But God doesn't forget them—and neither should we.

That nonverbal child may be worshiping God in ways we can't fully grasp. That child with autism may be more spiritually aware than we realize. That parent who hasn't heard a full sermon in years because they're always in the hallway with their child? They're heroes of the faith. These families aren't projects—they're people, loved deeply by God, and carrying stories of grace we need to hear.

Jesus never passed over children. He never said, "Come back when you're cleaner, quieter, or more mature." He welcomed them, blessed them, and saw them. And as His hands and feet today, we must do the same—especially for those whom the world too often looks past.

Let's do the same.

5. Understand That Suffering Doesn't Mean Rejection

It's hard to watch children suffer. It feels unfair. Why should the only godly person in a family get sick? Why do we see kids with disabilities, chronic illnesses, or struggles—while others seem to glide through life unaffected?

Spurgeon gives a compelling insight: sometimes, suffering is not a lack of God's love—but the very proof of it.

He says Abijah's sickness may have been like the bruising of a fig to ripen it. That he was taken early not as a punishment, but as a mercy—rescued from the evil to come.

That's deep theology for us, as adults—but it's also practical comfort. When we walk with kids through hard seasons, we must trust that God is still good. That He hasn't lost track of that child. And that even in pain, His grace is at work.

6. Trust God To Finish What He Starts

The phrase "some good thing" reminds me that we don't have to see everything for it to be real. We don't need a child to have perfect theology, memorize the entire Bible, or lead a revival at their school.

We just need to see that God has begun something.

Philippians 1:6 reminds us that the One who began a good work will carry it on to completion. If God has started "some good thing" in that boy or girl, He will keep working.

Our job is to come alongside, speak life, teach truth, and walk with them through the ups and downs of growing up in a complicated world. God will do the rest.

Final Thoughts

Spurgeon looked at the life of one little boy and found hope—not just for his time, but for all time. And if you're working with kids, I hope you find that same hope today.

Yes, the world is dark. Yes, many homes are broken. Yes, kids face things no child should ever face.

But if God could plant a "good thing" in the heart of a child in Jeroboam's palace, He can do it anywhere—even in the kids you serve.

So keep your eyes open. Keep your heart soft. Look for grace in unexpected places.

And when you find it—rejoice. Celebrate it. Nurture it.

You just may be looking at the next Abijah.

~ 22 ~

THE SHUNAMMITE WOMAN'S SON

L et me draw your attention to a very meaningful miracle performed by the prophet Elisha, as recorded in the Book of Kings. The kindness and hospitality of the Shunammite woman had been rewarded by the gift of a son; but, sadly, all earthly blessings are temporary, and after a few years, the child became sick and died.

The heartbroken but faith-filled mother immediately went to the man of God. Since the promise that brought her this child had come through him, she decided to bring her case to him, hoping he would bring it to his Divine Master and receive an answer of peace. Elisha's response is recorded in the following veres:

> Then he said to Gehazi, "Get ready, take my staff in your hand, and go. If you meet anyone, don't greet them, and if they greet you, don't answer back. Lay my staff on the child's face."

> But the child's mother said, "As surely as the Lord lives and as you live, I won't leave you." So he got up and followed her.

Gehazi went on ahead and laid the staff on the child's face, but there was no sound or response. So he went back to meet Elisha and told him, "The child hasn't woken up."

When Elisha came to the house, there was the child—dead, lying on his bed. He went in, shut the door behind the two of them, and prayed to the Lord. Then he got on the bed and lay on the child, mouth to mouth, eyes to eyes, hands to hands. As he stretched himself over the child, the boy's body grew warm.

Elisha turned away and walked back and forth in the room. Then he went back and stretched himself out on the child once more. The boy sneezed seven times and opened his eyes.

Elisha called Gehazi and said, 'Call the Shunammite woman.' So he did, and when she came in, Elisha said, 'Pick up your son.'

She came in, fell at his feet, and bowed to the ground. Then she took her son and went out."
—2 Kings 4:29–37

Elisha had to deal with a dead child. In this case, it was physical death. But the kind of death you and I face is just as real, even though it's spiritual. Boys and girls, just like adults, are "dead in their sins." It's essential that we fully understand this truth about humanity's natural condition. Unless you're completely convinced of the spiritual ruin and deadness of children, you won't be able to become a true blessing to them. Please approach them not as if they're just sleeping and need your words to wake them, but as spiritually lifeless, needing a miracle only God can perform. Elisha didn't settle for anything less than full restoration to life—and may you never settle for less than the salvation of eternal souls. Your mission isn't just to teach children to read the Bible, or to model good behavior, or even to explain the gospel message on the surface. Your calling is to be God's instrument to bring life from heaven into hearts that are spiritually dead.

Resurrection—that's the goal! To raise the spiritually dead—that's our mission! But how can we do something so impossible? If we let doubt creep in, we'll be overwhelmed by the fact that the work God has given us is way beyond our natural abilities. We can't raise the dead. But then again, neither could Elisha. That didn't discourage him, and it shouldn't discourage us. Instead, it should remind us where true power lies. I hope all of us understand by now that if you live in the world of faith, you're operating in the realm of miracles.

Elisha wasn't just any man—God's Spirit was on him, calling him to this work and empowering him for it. And you, faithful and prayerful teacher, are no longer just an ordinary person either. You are the temple of the Holy Spirit; God lives in you. And by faith, you've stepped into the role of a miracle worker. You've been sent into the world not to do the things that anyone can do, but to take part in the impossible things God does through His people. You're here to do wonders, to see miracles happen. So don't think that seeing spiritually dead children come to life is unlikely or difficult—remember who is working through you, even if you feel weak and ordinary.

It would've been better if Elisha had remembered that he once served Elijah and followed his example more closely. If he had, he wouldn't have sent Gehazi with the staff first—he would've done what he eventually had to do. If you read 1 Kings 17, you'll see how Elijah brought a dead child back to life, and you'll notice that Elisha finally did the same. It wasn't until Elisha followed Elijah's exact pattern that the miracle took place. It would've been wise for Elisha to imitate the example of his mentor. And it's even more important that we, as teachers, follow the example of our perfect Master—Jesus. Just as Jesus entered fully into our broken humanity and humbled Himself to meet us in our need, we must draw close to the children we serve. We need to feel what they feel, ache with their hurts, and love them with His love if we want to see them raised from sin. Only by reflecting the spirit and approach of Jesus can we be truly effective in winning souls.

I worry that sometimes the truth we teach is disconnected from who we are. It's like the staff Gehazi carried—it's in our hands, but it's not a part of us. We share Bible doctrines or moral lessons, stories or illustrations, but if those truths haven't gripped our hearts, they won't move the hearts of others. As long as we deliver truth as something outside of ourselves—something we speak without feeling or owning—it will have as little effect on a dead soul as Elisha's staff had on that lifeless child. We're not even sure Gehazi truly believed the child was dead. He seemed to think the child just needed to be woken up. But God won't bless teachers who don't see the reality of sin in the hearts of their students. If you believe children are naturally good, if you buy into the lie that they are innocent and pure by nature, don't be surprised when your ministry has no lasting fruit.

Look closely at what Elisha did after his first attempt failed. When one method didn't work, he didn't quit. And neither should we. If you've been teaching and haven't seen results, don't assume God hasn't called you. That's not what failure means. The message isn't "give up," but "try something else." Maybe your approach needs to change. Reflect on what hasn't worked. Try a different spirit, a deeper love, a more personal touch—and the Lord might use you in greater ways than you ever imagined. Elisha didn't lose heart when the child didn't respond. Instead, he rolled up his sleeves and threw himself into the work with renewed energy.

Reflections from Ryan

Bringing the Spiritually Dead to Life

The story of the Shunammite woman and her son is more than just an inspiring account from the Old Testament—it's a powerful picture of the calling that rests on our shoulders as children's ministry leaders and parents today. Charles Spurgeon reminds us that this child's physical death mirrors a deeper, more urgent reality: the spiritual death that exists in every heart until Jesus brings it to life.

That's a heavy truth—but it's also a hopeful one. Because it reminds us of why we do what we do.

Let's be real for a minute. Ministry to kids can feel exhausting. Parenting with purpose can be overwhelming. And in both spaces, it's easy to slip into a routine. We teach lessons. We plan services. We run events. We correct behavior. But Spurgeon, through Elisha's story, calls us back to our true mission: resurrection. We're not in this just to entertain or educate—we're here to see dead hearts brought to life by Jesus.

1. Let's Not Forget What's At Stake

Elisha wasn't called to make the dead boy feel more comfortable. He wasn't sent to teach him manners or keep him occupied. He was sent to bring life.

Parents, leaders—this is our mission too. Our kids don't just need good behavior, better grades, or fun experiences at church. They need Jesus. Desperately.

If we're not careful, we can fall into the trap of treating kids as if they're mostly good, just needing some direction. But Scripture says something very different. "Dead in sin" isn't a phrase reserved for hardened criminals or wayward adults—it's the condition of every child born into this world. Until Jesus brings them to life, they remain spiritually lifeless.

That might sound discouraging at first, but actually—it's clarifying. When we understand the seriousness of the need, we won't settle for surface-level ministry. We'll cry out to God for miracles. We'll give our best effort—not for entertainment, but for eternity.

2. Don't Settle For The Staff

I love Spurgeon's comparison of Gehazi's staff to our ministry tools. Think about it: the staff didn't wake the boy up. Why? Because the staff represented an external method disconnected from personal involvement. It was a "try this and see" approach—detached and mechanical.

How often do we do the same? We throw a curriculum at a kid. We quote a Bible verse and hope it sticks. We give them a piece of chocolate and move on.

But real life-change rarely happens that way. The Shunammite boy came back to life when Elisha stretched himself out, fully engaged— mouth to mouth, eye to eye, hand to hand. There was closeness, personal investment, and a deep awareness of the situation.

Ministry and parenting require that same kind of heart. If you want to see real transformation, it's not enough to just drop truth and walk away. You need to show up. Lean in. Feel what they feel. Love them deeply. Speak truth from your own experience, not just from a lesson plan.

You can't disciple from a distance.

3. Keep Going Even When Nothing Happens

Gehazi came back with a report no one wants to hear: "The child hasn't woken up." Translation: "It didn't work."

If you've been in children's ministry or parenting for any length of time, you've probably felt this. You teach faithfully, you pray consistently, you model Jesus—and… nothing. No breakthrough. No "aha" moment. No big God story.

But what did Elisha do? He didn't give up. He adjusted his approach. He went in personally, prayed fervently, and tried again.

Sometimes our first methods don't work. And that's okay. You don't need to throw in the towel—you need to try something different. Maybe your teaching style needs tweaking. Maybe you need to spend more one-on-one time with that child. Maybe you need to bring another leader into the situation. Or maybe you just need to pray harder and wait longer.

Faithful ministry is rarely flashy. It's often slow, and it almost always requires perseverance.

4. You're Not Powerless—You're Empowered

Elisha knew he couldn't raise the dead. But he also knew he didn't have to. That's God's job. His job was to show up in faith and obedience—and trust God to do the rest.

The same is true for you. You're not expected to save anyone. You're not expected to bring spiritual life through your own wisdom or charisma. You're expected to walk in faith, serve in love, and point kids to Jesus at every opportunity.

When you do that, the Spirit of God works through you—yes, you—to do the impossible.

Don't downplay your role. You may feel ordinary, but if you're filled with the Holy Spirit and surrendered to God, you're anything but. You are part of heaven's rescue mission in the life of every child you influence.

5. Pray Like Elisha—And Then Some

One of the most overlooked parts of this story is how Elisha prayed. Before he stretched himself over the boy, he shut the door and prayed to the Lord.

Prayer was his first move—not the last resort.

We'd do well to follow that example. If we want to see resurrection power at work in our kids, we need to go to our knees first. Pray for the kids in your ministry by name. Pray for the spiritual climate in your home. Ask God for open hearts, for divine encounters, and for breakthrough moments.

And don't stop praying when things look lifeless. Pray until something shifts. Pray until warmness returns to cold hearts. Pray until you see eyes open.

Final Thoughts

I love how the story ends: the boy opened his eyes, and then Elisha said, "Take up your son." Can you imagine that moment? The mother runs in, falls at Elisha's feet in awe, and then scoops her living child into her arms.

That's what we're praying and working for—that moment when a child we've poured into finally "gets it," finally sees Jesus, finally comes alive. Whether it happens at VBS, during bedtime devotions, or in the middle of a quiet worship moment—that's why we do this.

Don't lose heart. Stay the course. The same God who raised the Shunammite's son is still bringing dead hearts to life—and He's chosen to use you in the process.

Let's get back to resurrection work. Let's love deeply, pray boldly, and lead faithfully.

~ 23 ~

THE SHUNAMMITE WOMAN'S SON—PART 2

Notice where the dead child was placed: "And when Elisha came into the house, he saw that the child was dead and lying on his bed." This was the bed that the Shunammite woman had set up for Elisha out of her hospitality—the famous bed that, along with the table, chair, and lamp, has become unforgettable in the church of God.

As we continue reading, we find, "He went in, therefore, and shut the door behind them both, and prayed to the Lord." Now the prophet gets down to serious work, and we're given a powerful example of how to raise children from spiritual death. If you turn back to the story of Elijah, you'll find that Elisha followed the tried-and-true method used by his mentor. It says, "He said to her, 'Give me your son.' So he took him from her arms and carried him to the upstairs room where he was staying, and laid him on his own bed. He cried out to the Lord and said, 'O Lord my God, have you brought tragedy on this widow I'm staying with, by killing her son?' Then he stretched himself out over the boy three times and cried to the Lord, 'O Lord my God, please let this boy's life return to him!' The Lord heard Elijah's cry, and the boy's life returned to him, and he lived."

The main key here is passionate prayer. "He shut the door behind them both and prayed to the Lord." There's an old saying: "Every real pulpit is built in heaven," meaning that a true preacher spends serious time with God. If we don't ask God for His blessing—if we don't build our public ministry on private prayer—it won't be effective. The same goes for you. Any real power in teaching must come from above. If you never go into your private room and shut the door behind you, if you never plead at God's mercy seat for your child, how can you expect God to bless you with their salvation?

One great way to do this is to take the children one by one into your room and pray with them. You'll see change when you start praying for them individually—when you feel deep burden for them and plead with God behind closed doors. One-on-one prayer can be far more impactful than even the most powerful public prayers in class—not necessarily more powerful to God, but more powerful to the child. That kind of prayer can often bring about its own answer, because God might use your heartfelt prayer to break a child's heart that sermons couldn't reach.

After praying, Elisha took action. Prayer and action must go hand in hand. Action without prayer? That's arrogance. Prayer without action? That's hypocrisy.

There lay the child, and there stood the man of God. Watch how he moves: he leans over the child and places his mouth on the boy's mouth. The prophet's warm breath entered the lifeless mouth, throat, and lungs. Then, full of love and hope, Elisha placed his eyes over the child's eyes and his hands over the child's hands—his warm hands covering the cold ones. Then he stretched himself out over the child completely, as if he were trying to give his own life to the lifeless body—willing either to die with the child or to make him live.

We've heard of the mountain guide who, when taking a nervous traveler across a dangerous ridge, tied them together and said, "Both or neither." That's what Elisha was doing—he united himself to the child as if saying, "We rise or fall together."

What does this teach us? So much. It shows us that if we want to bring spiritual life to a child, we must deeply understand their condition. They are dead—dead in sin. God wants you to feel the weight of that. You must enter into the reality of their spiritual death with heartfelt, humbling sympathy.

If you want to win souls, follow Jesus' example. What did He do to raise us from the dead? He died Himself. That's the way. If you want to reach a spiritually dead child, you must feel the coldness and fear of their death yourself. You must experience, to some degree, the fear of God's wrath and the reality of coming judgment. If you don't, your work will lack urgency—and that urgency is essential for success. I don't believe any preacher ever speaks well of such things unless he feels them deep in his soul.

John Bunyan once said, "I preached in chains to men in chains." In the same way, when the lost condition of your children weighs heavily on you, when it distresses and burdens you, then you can expect God to move.

After realizing the child's condition and placing your mouth on their mouth, and your hands on theirs, you must also work to relate to them—to understand their thoughts, their habits, their personalities. You have to speak their language, see things through their eyes, feel what they feel, and be a true friend.

You must study the kinds of sins children struggle with. You must care about their trials. You must enter their world of joys and sorrows. Don't let the difficulty discourage you. If something hard is needed, then do it—without complaining. God won't raise a child through you unless you're willing to meet them where they are, however inconvenient or humbling it may be.

The prophet "stretched himself out over the child." You might think it should say "he shrank himself," since he was a grown man and the child was small. But no—it says "he stretched himself," and that's exactly right. Nothing is harder than stretching yourself to a child's level.

It takes wisdom, deep thought, hard work, and prayer to really teach children. It's not for the lazy or the shallow. The best minds and the most caring hearts are needed to guide young souls.

So with Elisha we see an awareness of the child's need, a willingness to meet him where he is, and—above all—real, heartfelt sympathy. As Elisha lay there, his own warmth entered the child's body. That warmth didn't bring life on its own, but God used it as part of the process.

Let every teacher consider Paul's words: "But we were gentle among you, like a nursing mother cherishes her children. So we loved you so much that we were happy to share not only the gospel with you, but our very lives, because you had become so dear to us." God will bless this kind of loving, sacrificial spirit in teaching. The truth, spoken with deep love, can do what truth alone cannot.

This is the secret: you must pour out your soul for the children. Their spiritual ruin must feel like your own.

Soon the result came: "The child's body grew warm." Elisha must have rejoiced—but he didn't stop there. Don't settle for seeing your students become merely interested or touched. What you want is not just awareness but true transformation. Not just a stir in the heart, but new life from Jesus. That's what your kids need—nothing less will do.

"Then he got up and walked back and forth in the house." See how restless Elisha is—he can't sit still. The child's body is warm (thank God), but he isn't alive yet. So Elisha walks back and forth, unsettled, praying, yearning, burdened. He can't bear to face the grieving mother or answer her questions. Instead, he paces the house, because his heart is still crying out.

Follow this example of holy restlessness. If you see signs of awakening in a child, don't sit back and say, "That's good enough." You won't win eternal souls with a casual attitude. You need to care deeply, to the point of discomfort, if you want to be a spiritual parent.

After pacing, the prophet went up again and "stretched himself out over the child." What's worth doing once is worth doing again—and again. Good efforts should be repeated. Persistence and patience are essential. Just as Elisha's warmth flowed into the child, your spiritual coldness can also affect your students if you lose your passion.

Elisha stretched out again—praying, sighing, believing—and finally his request was granted. "The child sneezed seven times and opened his eyes."

Any sign of life would have thrilled the prophet. Some say the child died of a head illness, because he had cried, "My head! My head!"—so the sneezing may have cleared his airways. Either way, the sneeze showed life had returned.

It wasn't eloquent or dramatic, but it was enough. And when it comes to spiritual life in children, this is often what we get. Some church members expect something big—but I'm happy if a child just "sneezes"—any sincere sign of spiritual awakening, no matter how small.

If Gehazi had been there, he might not have thought much of it—he hadn't laid on the child. But Elisha understood. Likewise, when you and I have truly wept and prayed for a soul, we'll be quick to notice even the faintest signs of grace and give God thanks.

Then the child opened his eyes—and I'm sure Elisha thought they were the most beautiful eyes he'd ever seen. Whether they were blue or hazel doesn't matter. Any eye God uses you to open will be the most beautiful eye in the world.

Reflections from Ryan

Keep Stretching

There are moments in ministry—especially in children's ministry—when we feel helpless. We see kids struggling with real pain, confusion, and spiritual emptiness. And let's be honest: it can feel like we're staring at lifeless situations. That's why this story of Elisha and the Shunammite's son hits me so hard. It's not just about a boy being physically raised from the dead; it's a spiritual picture of what God wants to do through us as we minister to the next generation.

I believe Spurgeon's unpacking of this story holds gold for us today. If you're a parent, pastor, KidMin leader, or volunteer, there's something here for you. Let's take a deep breath and walk through it together.

1. It Starts In Private Prayer

Elisha didn't rush into action. He shut the door and prayed. In today's world of fast-paced programs, social media posts, and Pinterest-worthy activities, it's easy to skip the foundation. But Spurgeon reminds us—no matter how excellent your teaching, how creative your environments, or how dynamic your volunteers—if your ministry isn't built on prayer, it's built on sand.

Parents, when was the last time you prayed privately, by name, for each of your kids? Ministry leaders, when was the last time you interceded for the child who tests your patience the most?

If we want God to bring life to the spiritually dead, we must be people of private prayer. Prayer that's specific. Prayer that's desperate. Prayer that shuts the door and says, "God, I won't leave until You move."

2. Ministry Requires Contact

Elisha didn't raise the boy by preaching at him from across the room. He got close. He stretched himself out over the child. It's a strange image, but it speaks volumes: real ministry requires contact. We must be willing to engage with children's lives on their level.

This isn't just about being in the room—it's about being present. It's about asking questions, listening to answers, showing up at their soccer games, remembering their birthdays, and being the kind of adult they can trust. This kind of ministry is messy, inconvenient, and uncomfortable—but it's the kind that leads to transformation.

If you only feel called to the stage and not to the classroom, you may be missing your true calling. Jesus came close to us. And if we want to see kids come to life, we must come close to them.

3. You Have to Stretch Yourself

I love how Spurgeon points this out. He says it should have said Elisha contracted himself to fit the child—but instead, the Word says he stretched himself. Wow. That speaks to the real cost of ministry today.

If you want to impact the next generation, you will have to stretch.

You will stretch your time. Your patience. Your understanding. Your comfort zones. You will stretch the way you communicate so kids can grasp deep truth. You'll stretch your imagination to make the gospel come alive. And sometimes, you'll stretch your heart so wide it hurts.

But this stretching is where the power is. It's where the life flows. Kids don't need leaders who tower over them—they need leaders who will meet them where they are.

4. Feel What They Feel

Elisha didn't just lay on the boy—he gave his warmth. There's no shortcut here. We must feel what our kids feel. Empathy is not a buzzword—it's a requirement. If we're going to reach a generation bombarded by anxiety, identity confusion, and brokenness at younger and younger ages, we have to feel the weight of what they're carrying.

We must ask God to burden our hearts for the kids we teach. We must look at them not as "someone else's problem" but as souls we are personally responsible to care for.

You can't heal what you don't care about. And you won't care unless you allow yourself to enter into their pain.

5. Don't Settle For "Warm"

One of my favorite parts of this passage is that Elisha didn't stop when the child's body got warm. He could have walked away and said, "Hey, progress!" But warm wasn't enough. The boy needed to live.

Too often in ministry, we settle for emotional reactions or temporary interest. We celebrate attendance without transformation. We're excited when a child "sits still" or "participates"—but friends, warm is not alive.

We must keep pressing until we see real evidence of new life. Not just behavior change, but heart change. Not just kids who know answers, but kids who know Jesus. Don't rest until your kids open their eyes.

6. Restlessness Is Holy

Elisha walked the room, restless and unsettled. He wasn't satisfied. I believe that kind of holy restlessness is missing in many ministries. We're too quick to declare victory and move on.

If you're truly called, you won't be able to relax when your kids are lost. When you see one wandering, your heart should ache. You'll pace the room. You'll skip sleep. You'll fast. You'll cry. This is what spiritual parenting looks like.

Let God put a fresh fire in you—a discontentment with the status quo. Until every child in your care truly lives, don't be still.

7. Watch For The Sneezes

When the child sneezed, it may have seemed small. But to Elisha, it was everything. He knew what that sneeze meant—it meant life had returned.

Sometimes we look for big, flashy signs of God working. But don't miss the sneezes. Don't miss when a kid asks a thoughtful question, invited a friend to church, brings their Bible, or sings a worship song for the first time. Those little "sneezes" might just be the early signs of spiritual life.

Celebrate the small steps. Notice what others overlook. If you've prayed and labored, you'll spot grace even in the simplest signs.

8. The Eyes That Open Are Beautiful

Finally, Elisha saw the child's eyes open—and he must have thought they were the most beautiful eyes in the world. That's how I feel when I see a child come to Jesus. When I see the light turn on. When I hear their prayers, their childlike faith, and their desire to follow Him—it's beautiful. There's nothing like it.

You can build big programs and chase big goals, but if you lose sight of the individual child who comes to life in Christ, you've missed the point.

Don't forget: every child is a soul. Every soul matters to God. And God wants to use you—yes, you—to help raise them to life.

Let's Keep Stretching

Friends, let's not be content with good intentions or warm classrooms. Let's be ministers who stretch. Who pray. Who connect. Who empathize. Who notice the sneezes and keep praying until the eyes open.

You may never lay across a dead body like Elisha, but you lay across spiritual death every day when you step into your ministry calling. May

God give you the grace, the passion, and the power to stretch—and may He raise a generation to life through you.

You're not alone. You're not weak. You're called.

And the eyes that open will be more beautiful than you can imagine.

Let's Keep Going—Together

If you've made it to this final chapter, let me begin with a heartfelt thank you. I'm so glad you chose to take this journey through Charles Spurgeon's *Come Ye Children* with me. My hope and prayer is that you have found deep encouragement, timeless wisdom, and renewed clarity about the calling God has placed on your life to minister to children.

Rewriting this book in modern English and reflecting on each chapter has been a deeply personal and spiritual experience for me. As I worked through Spurgeon's original words, I often found myself amazed at how relevant his thoughts still are today. In fact, in many ways, they feel more urgent now than ever before. The culture around us is rapidly shifting. Families are facing unprecedented pressures. And children are being pulled in countless directions. Now is the time to double down on our commitment to reach the hearts of kids with the hope of Jesus.

Spurgeon's words reminded me over and over again just how vital, urgent, and powerful children's ministry truly is. The truths he shared more than a century ago still ring true today, and I'm convinced that they need to be heard by every parent, pastor, teacher, and ministry leader who has said yes to serving the next generation.

Children's ministry is sacred work. It is often unseen, sometimes exhausting, and frequently underappreciated—but it matters so deeply. The seeds you plant today may not bear fruit tomorrow, but they will grow. God sees your efforts. He sees every diaper changed, every Bible story told, every craft prepared, and every prayer whispered over a child's life. He sees your consistency when others don't. And He promises that your labor in the Lord is never in vain.

Over the years, I've met thousands of KidMin leaders across the country. I've listened to their stories. I've heard their challenges and celebrated their victories. And I've learned this: the best children's ministry leaders are not necessarily the ones with the biggest budgets or the fanciest rooms. They're the ones who show up—week after week—with love, faithfulness, and a heart to make a difference in the life of a child.

At KidzMatter, our mission is simple: to equip and encourage the global children's ministry community. That includes you. Whether you're a volunteer at a small church or a full-time children's pastor at a large campus, we want you to know that you're not alone. We are in your corner, and we want to come alongside you every step of the way.

We often say that KidzMatter exists to help leaders win in ministry and in life. Because both matter. You can't separate the health of your ministry from the health of your soul. That's why our approach is holistic. Yes, we provide resources, training, and tools—but we also offer encouragement, prayer, and personal support. We believe in who you are and what you've been called to do.

We believe that strong kids' ministries don't just happen by accident—they are built by intentional leaders who are resourced, refreshed, and supported. And you don't have to figure it all out on your own. That's where we come in.

Let me take a moment to share just a few ways KidzMatter can continue to serve and support you beyond this book.

THE KIDZMATTER CONFERENCE

In just a short number of years, The KidzMatter Conference has grown to become the largest gathering of children's ministry leaders in the United States. Every fall, thousands of leaders from all over the country gather for an experience that goes far beyond what you might expect from a typical ministry conference.

It's a family reunion where you reconnect with old friends and make new ones who truly understand the calling of children's ministry. It's a spiritual reset, providing moments of worship, prayer, and encouragement that breathe fresh life into your soul. It's a training ground, filled with breakout sessions, mainstage teaching, and creative resources that equip you to grow your ministry with excellence and passion.

At the KidzMatter Conference, you'll be surrounded by people who get you—leaders who have wiped the same noses, prayed over the same empty chairs, and celebrated the same small victories. You'll be equipped by dynamic speakers who are not only skilled communicators but who also carry a deep love for Jesus and for the next generation. You'll be refreshed by worship that lifts your spirit and recenters your heart. And you'll be encouraged by leaders and peers who understand the unique challenges and joys of your calling.

If you've never attended, we'd love for you to make this the year you join us. Come and see what God can do when KidMin leaders come together to learn, grow, and lift each other up. It just might be the spark your ministry needs. People consistently leave the conference saying they feel seen, celebrated, and spiritually renewed—and that's exactly our heart.

KIDMIN
ACADEMY

If you're looking for more in-depth training and development, KidMin Academy is for you. This isn't just an online course—it's a transformational learning experience built specifically for children's ministry leaders. Whether you're brand-new to ministry or have years of experience, KidMin Academy offers valuable training that meets you right where you are.

The program provides comprehensive, biblically grounded ministry training in a flexible online format. That means you can learn at your own pace, on your own schedule, without having to hit pause on your current responsibilities. The lessons are taught by experienced ministry practitioners who have been in the trenches and understand the real-world challenges you face.

You'll explore topics like volunteer recruitment and training, classroom management, spiritual formation, leadership development, communication with parents, event planning, and more. But it's not just about gaining information—it's about transformation. You'll develop the confidence, clarity, and competence needed to lead a thriving ministry.

Through KidMin Academy, you'll also be part of a growing community of fellow learners and leaders. You'll find encouragement, share ideas, and build relationships that last beyond the classroom. Many graduates have gone on to take their ministries to new levels and even train others on their teams.

Best of all, KidMin Academy is rooted in the belief that your personal growth is just as important as your professional development. We care about your heart, your walk with Jesus, and your long-term sustainability in ministry.

KIDZMATTER
MAGAZINE

There's something powerful about holding a printed magazine in your hands, flipping through its pages, and finding inspiration, ideas, and encouragement. In a world dominated by screens and digital overload, there's still something refreshing and grounding about engaging with content that's thoughtfully curated and beautifully designed—on paper. That's why we continue to publish KidzMatter Magazine—and now, it's absolutely free.

Each issue of the magazine is filled with real stories from leaders like you, practical tips you can use this Sunday, and proven strategies to help you lead your team and reach your kids more effectively. We cover topics like leadership development, creative teaching techniques, team building, family ministry, and navigating the everyday challenges of ministry life. It's written by people who get what you do and care deeply about your success.

And it's more than just good content. KidzMatter Magazine is a visual experience. We work hard to make sure it's not only useful but also beautiful and fun to read. From inspiring articles to full-page game ideas and ministry tools, it's something you'll want to pick up again and again.

It's also an incredible resource to share with your volunteers and church staff. Many leaders tell us they keep stacks of back issues in their office or volunteer rooms—ready to pass along an article, spark a discussion, or provide a dose of encouragement to someone on their team.

At www.kidzmatter.com/magazine you can request your free print subscription. We would love to send you the latest issue and help you stay equipped and encouraged all year long.

Want access to even more resources all year long? KidzMatter PRO is our monthly membership program designed to keep your ministry fueled, focused, and fresh—week in and week out. It's the go-to toolbox for children's ministry leaders who want to stay sharp, inspired, and equipped.

Each month, KidzMatter PRO members receive exclusive digital downloads, on-screen games, training tools, curriculum helps, templates, leadership coaching, and more. Whether you need a new game for Sunday morning, a last-minute parent handout, or a leadership checklist for your volunteers—PRO has your back. And it's not just random content—it's purposeful, high-quality material created with real ministry in mind.

In addition to resources, PRO includes live coaching and access to monthly masterclasses where we dive deep into ministry topics and offer practical solutions. You'll be able to ask questions, get feedback, and grow alongside a community of fellow leaders who understand your world.

Many leaders describe KidzMatter PRO as their "secret weapon." It's like having a personal coach, creative team, and resource library all in one easy-to-access platform. And because we update the content every single month, there's always something new to spark ideas and breathe life into your ministry routines.

KidzMatter PRO isn't just about convenience—it's about confidence. It's about giving you the tools you need to lead well, disciple effectively, and avoid burnout. It helps you show up prepared, encouraged, and inspired—week after week.

Plus, PRO members receive exclusive discounts on products, priority access to events, and special behind-the-scenes content you won't find anywhere else.

If you're ready to take your ministry leadership to the next level, we'd love to welcome you into the PRO community!

Say Hello to KidzMatter

And if you're just discovering KidzMatter, we want to welcome you in a special way. We'd love to send you our "Say Hello to KidzMatter: Your Ministry Friend" welcome box—a free gift from us to you. This isn't just a box of stuff—it's a box of encouragement, packed with tools, resources, and surprises created with your ministry in mind.

Inside, you'll find the KidzMatter Magazine, filled with stories, tips, and encouragement from real ministry leaders like you. You'll also receive The KidzMatter Playbook, a guide filled with practical strategies to help you lead your ministry with purpose and passion. We've included a KidMin Academy journal so you can reflect, take notes, and track your ministry goals. And because we like surprises, we've added a couple of bonus goodies that we think will bring a smile to your face.

This box is our way of saying, "Welcome to the family." We know that starting something new or stepping into a new season of ministry can feel overwhelming. That's why we want to come alongside you from the very beginning and remind you that you don't have to do this alone.

The best part? It's completely free. We just ask that you cover the cost of shipping. At www.kidzmatter.com/hello you can request your welcome box and we'll get it in the mail right away.

If you're ready to explore what KidzMatter has to offer—or if you just need a little boost to keep going—we hope this welcome package will be a blessing to you. We believe in what God is doing through you, and we'd be honored to be a part of your journey.

Final Thoughts

We believe that every KidMin leader should have someone in their corner. That's what we want to be for you. No matter where you serve, what size your ministry is, or how long you've been in the trenches—your work matters, and you deserve support, encouragement, and community.

Ministry can feel lonely sometimes. There are seasons where you feel like no one understands the weight you carry. Maybe you're pouring yourself out week after week and wondering if it's really making a difference. Maybe you're in a place of transition or rebuilding. Or maybe you're leading through exciting growth and need wisdom on how to steward what God is doing. Whatever your season, we want to remind you: you don't have to walk this road alone.

At KidzMatter, we believe ministry is meant to be done in community. It's more fun, more fruitful, and far more fulfilling when we walk together. That's why we do what we do. That's why we create resources, host conferences, publish magazines, and build coaching programs—because we believe in the leaders behind the ministry.

Beth and I talk often about how honored we feel to serve you. This isn't just a job to us. It's a calling. We genuinely care about your heart, your family, your team, and your spiritual health. We think about you when we're designing resources. We pray for you as we plan events. And we celebrate with you when we hear stories of how God is using your ministry to impact kids and families.

Please don't hesitate to reach out. If there's anything we can do to serve you, encourage you, pray with you, or simply listen—we're here. You can reach me directly at ryan@kidzmatter.com and Beth at beth@kidzmatter.com. We'd love to hear from you. Even if it's just to say hello or share how God is working in your corner of the world.

You matter. Your work matters. Your calling matters. And you don't have to do it alone.

We're cheering for you.

We believe in you.

We thank God for you.

Now, let's keep going—together.

The Most Important Invitation

If you've read this far, you already know: this book is about much more than ministry tips, volunteer training, or children's ministry ideas. At its heart, it's about Jesus. Every story, every lesson, every reflection—all of it points back to Him. Because without Jesus, we have nothing to offer the next generation. But with Jesus? We have everything.

So let me ask you a personal question: Do you know Him?

I don't mean "know about Him." I mean—have you placed your trust in Him? Has there been a moment in your life when you turned from sin and chose to follow Jesus?

It's easy to assume that everyone reading a book like this already has a relationship with Christ. But sometimes, especially in ministry, we get so busy helping others walk with Jesus that we forget to stop and ask: Have I truly begun that walk myself?

Or maybe you're reading this because someone handed it to you—a friend, a pastor, a parent—and you're curious about what it really means to follow God. Maybe you've grown up around the Church but never made a personal decision. Maybe you've been distant from God for a long time and aren't sure how to come back.

Whatever your story is—this page is for you.

God Made You For A Relationship With Him

The Bible tells us that we were created in the image of God. That means you are not an accident. You're not here by chance. You were made on purpose, for a purpose—designed to walk in relationship with your Creator.

But something stands in the way of that relationship. It's called sin. Sin is more than just "messing up" or doing bad things—it's our decision to live life our own way instead of God's way. The Bible says that "all have sinned and fall short of the glory of God" (Romans 3:23). That includes you and me.

The problem with sin is that it separates us from God. And no amount of good deeds, religious effort, or positive thinking can bridge that gap. Sin carries a penalty—eternal separation from God. But the good news of the gospel is this: Jesus came to rescue us.

Jesus Did What We Couldn't

Jesus is God's Son. He came to earth, lived a perfect and sinless life, and then willingly went to the cross to take the punishment for our sin. He died in our place. But He didn't stay dead—He rose again three days later, proving His power over sin and death.

The Bible says, "God demonstrates his own love for us in this: While we were still sinners, Christ died for us" (Romans 5:8).

That's the message of the gospel: We couldn't save ourselves, so Jesus did it for us. His death paid the price. His resurrection opened the door. And now, eternal life is available to anyone who believes.

That includes you.

What Does It Mean to Be Saved?

Salvation isn't about trying harder, being religious, or cleaning up your act before you come to God. It's about surrender. It's about putting your faith in Jesus—trusting that His death and resurrection are enough to cover your sin and give you new life.

Romans 10:9 says, "If you confess with your mouth, 'Jesus is Lord,' and believe in your heart that God raised Him from the dead, you will be saved."

It's that simple. Not easy—but simple. Believe. Confess. Receive.

When you trust in Jesus, something amazing happens. Your sins are forgiven. You are made new. The Holy Spirit comes to live inside you. You are adopted into God's family. And you are promised eternal life—not just someday in heaven, but right now, as you walk daily with Him.

Would You Like to Make That Decision Today?

If you've never made the decision to follow Jesus—or if you're not sure—there's no better time than right now. You don't need fancy words or a perfect background. You just need a heart that's ready to say yes.

Here's a simple prayer you can pray. It's not magic, but if these words reflect what's in your heart, God will hear you:

Dear Jesus, I know that I've sinned and I need You. I believe that You died on the cross for my sins and rose again. Right now, I turn from my sin and place my trust in You alone. Please forgive me, change me, and help me live for You. I want to follow You from this day forward. Thank You for loving me. Amen.

If you prayed that prayer and meant it, welcome to the family of God. Heaven is rejoicing—and so are we!

If You're Helping a Child Take This Step

Since this book is also for children's ministry leaders and parents, I want to offer a word of encouragement: You can lead a child to Jesus.

Sometimes adults feel intimidated by the idea of guiding a child through a salvation decision. But the gospel is simple enough for a child to understand. If a child is showing interest in Jesus, asking spiritual questions, or expressing a desire to follow Him—lean into it.

Explain the gospel in clear, age-appropriate language. Ask questions to check for understanding. Don't rush them—but don't hold them back either. And remember, salvation is a work of the Holy Spirit, not our persuasive skills. Trust God to lead their heart.

If a child makes a decision to follow Jesus, celebrate it! Write down the date. Tell their family. Talk about baptism. Begin the discipleship process. This isn't the finish line—it's the starting point of a new life with Jesus.

What's Next?

If you or someone you know just placed their faith in Jesus, don't walk this new road alone. Tell someone. Find a Bible-believing church. Start reading God's Word—begin with the Gospel of John. Begin praying each day. Surround yourself with others who will encourage and challenge you in your faith.

And if there's anything we at KidzMatter can do to help you on this journey—reach out. We're not just here for ministry leaders. We're here for anyone who wants to walk with Jesus and help others do the same.

Email me at ryan@kidzmatter.com. I'd love to hear your story, celebrate your decision, and support you however we can.

You Matter to God

I'll close with this: God loves you. He made you. He sent His Son for you. And He's inviting you into a relationship that will change your life forever.

Don't wait. Don't wonder. Say yes to Jesus today.

Because in the end, this book, this ministry, this life—it's all about Him.

A Final Commissioning Prayer & Blessing

Heavenly Father,

Thank You for the honor of serving Your children. I don't take it lightly. You have entrusted me with something sacred: the opportunity to lead, teach, and love the next generation in Your name.

Today, I respond to Your call to "Feed My lambs." I say yes.

I give You my hands—may they serve with care, create with joy, and offer comfort.

I give You my feet—may they go wherever You lead, even when it's hard or unfamiliar.

I give You my voice—may it speak truth, encouragement, and the good news of Jesus with clarity and love.

I give You my heart—may it remain soft and fully surrendered, even when ministry is messy.

And I give You my mind—may it stay fixed on You and the mission You've placed before me.

Jesus, fill me so I can pour out.

I can't feed others if I'm spiritually starving. Help me to prioritize time in Your Word, in prayer, and in Your presence—not out of obligation, but because I'm Your child too. May my leadership be an overflow of intimacy with You.

Let my life reflect what I teach. Let my example speak louder than my words. And let the kids I serve see someone who truly loves You—not just on Sundays, but every day.

When I'm tired, give me strength.

When I feel unseen, remind me You see.

When I celebrate, keep me humble.

When I want to quit, give me fresh vision.

Remind me often why I started. Remind me who I'm serving. Remind me that You're with me.

Give me eyes to see each child as You do—created in Your image, full of potential, worthy of love. Help me to love the quiet ones, the loud ones, the leaders, the wanderers, the ones who ask hard questions, and the ones with special needs. Let no child feel invisible in the space I lead.

Help me to create environments where kids feel safe, seen, and spiritually nourished. Remind me that my calling is not to entertain—but to equip. Not to impress—but to invest. Not to go viral—but to be faithful.

When ministry feels small or slow, remind me that eternity is being shaped in those moments. When I teach a Bible story, when I sit with a hurting child, when I wipe down tables or stay late to lock up—remind me it all matters to You.

You see. You reward. You're working.

I bless the children I serve. May they come to know You early and follow You always. May their hearts be tender, their minds be open, and their lives be used for Your glory.

I bless my fellow leaders and teammates. May we serve with unity, patience, humility, and joy. May we cheer one another on, carry each other's burdens, and grow stronger together.

Lord, help me lead in love.

Help me teach with truth.

Help me live with integrity.

Let me be known not for what I do—but for who I reflect.

Let it all point to Jesus.

When I feel discouraged, remind me that I'm part of something much bigger than I see. I join a long line of faithful servants—pastors, parents, volunteers, missionaries—who said "yes" to discipling children, trusting You for the results.

Whether I see fruit today or not until heaven, help me stay faithful.

Help me plant, water, and believe for the harvest.

Use my life. Use my words. Use my love.

For every child, every family, and every generation still to come.

I end this book where I began—with a heart full of gratitude and a spirit ready to serve.

Lord, I am Yours.

I am called.

I am equipped.

I am commissioned.

Let me feed Your lambs well.

In Jesus' name,

Amen.

Reflection Questions for You & Your Team

Use these questions to pause, pray, and process the powerful messages found throughout *Come Ye Children*. Whether you're a parent seeking to shepherd your children well, a volunteer investing in kids week after week, or a full-time children's ministry leader carrying the weight of spiritual formation for many, these prompts are designed to stir your heart and sharpen your focus.

Reflection is a vital part of spiritual growth—it allows us to slow down, listen to the Holy Spirit, and align our lives more closely with God's calling. As you work through each question, take time to journal your thoughts, talk with your team, or even pray through your responses. These aren't just questions to fill space; they are invitations to deeper insight, renewed passion, and greater faithfulness. Let them challenge your thinking, affirm your calling, and reignite your commitment to discipling the next generation with purpose and love.

Chapter 1: The Importance of Childlike Faith

1. What do I believe about the spiritual capacity of children?
2. Have I ever underestimated what God can do through a child?
3. How am I cultivating childlike faith in my own walk with Jesus?
4. What does our church or ministry communicate about the value of kids?
5. Are we prioritizing children in our church calendar, budget, and leadership conversations?

Chapter 2: The Value of Early Instruction

1. Am I intentionally investing in spiritual formation during the early years?
2. What habits or routines could help build a stronger spiritual foundation for our children?
3. Who influenced my spiritual development as a child—and how can I be that person for someone else?
4. Are our teaching methods engaging enough for young minds?
5. How are we equipping parents to be the primary disciplers in the home?

Chapter 3: Let the Children Come

1. Do I have any "grown-up" biases that unintentionally hinder kids from encountering Jesus?
2. How can our ministry be more welcoming to children from broken or unchurched homes?
3. Are there any barriers in our church that might prevent children from feeling like they belong?
4. In what ways are we "blessing" children the way Jesus did?
5. How do we demonstrate that the gospel is just as much for them as it is for adults?

Chapter 4: Why We Must Teach Children Now

1. What am I doing now that is planting seeds for the future?
2. Are there any moments or opportunities I'm currently wasting that could be redeemed for kingdom impact?
3. How can we better seize the spiritual openness of childhood?
4. In what ways are we preparing kids not just for today—but for life?
5. What might happen if we delay teaching truth to the next generation?

Chapter 5: The Child is Not Too Young to Learn

1. What adjustments do I need to make in how I communicate spiritual truths to young kids?
2. Have I overlooked anyone because I assumed they were "too young" or "not ready"?
3. How do I gauge spiritual responsiveness in the children I serve?
4. Do I believe that even preschoolers can grasp the love of God?
5. Are our leaders equipped to teach younger children with clarity and confidence?

Chapter 6: Expect God to Work in Kids' Lives

1. Am I praying bold prayers for the children in my life?
2. Do my teaching prep and volunteer training reflect high spiritual expectations?
3. What stories of God working in kids' lives can I celebrate and share?
4. How do we handle children's spiritual questions and expressions of faith?
5. Are we encouraging kids to respond to God—even if they don't yet have the vocabulary for it?

Chapter 7: Be Bold in Teaching Truth

1. Am I sugarcoating the gospel or watering it down for kids?
2. How do we balance simplicity with theological depth in our lessons?
3. Do our kids know what sin is, why we need Jesus, and how to follow Him?
4. How confident are our teachers in sharing the plan of salvation?
5. What's one area of truth we need to teach more clearly or consistently?

Chapter 8: The Spirit Can Work in a Child's Heart

1. Am I allowing space for the Holy Spirit to move in our services?
2. How often do I pray for spiritual breakthroughs in our kids' lives?
3. Do I trust God to do the work—or am I trying to force results?
4. What might the Spirit be doing in a child's heart right now that I don't see?
5. How are we helping kids listen for God's voice?

Chapter 9: Show Them Jesus

1. Am I pointing kids to Jesus—or just to behavior improvement?
2. What part of Jesus' life or character do our kids know best?
3. In what ways can we help kids build a personal friendship with Jesus?
4. Do I speak more about rules or about relationship?
5. How can I reflect Jesus better in my own attitude and actions?

Chapter 10: Salvation Is for Children Too

1. Do I believe that a child's faith can be genuine and lasting?
2. How do we validate and celebrate children's spiritual milestones?
3. Are we tracking and following up on decisions for Christ?
4. What does our ministry "next step" path look like for kids?
5. Do we create space for testimonies from kids?

Chapter 11: The Power of a Child's Prayer

1. When was the last time I learned something about prayer from a child?
2. How do we encourage children to pray on their own?
3. Are we modeling passionate, personal prayer?
4. What can we do to create more prayer moments in our services or homes?
5. Do we pray with children or only for them?

Chapter 12: Teach Morality but Emphasize Grace

1. Are we teaching good behavior without the gospel?
2. How do we emphasize that salvation is by grace—not works?
3. Do our kids understand the why behind God's commands?
4. How do we help children apply biblical truth to everyday choices?
5. In what ways are we communicating that God's love is not based on performance?

Chapter 13: Keep the Audience in Mind

1. Do we understand our kids' life stage, culture, and learning needs?
2. Are our lessons engaging and age-appropriate?
3. How can we become better listeners of the kids we serve?
4. What might our teaching look like through a child's eyes?
5. Are we involving kids in ministry decisions that affect them?

Chapter 14: Diamonds in the Dust

1. Who are the overlooked kids in our ministry?
2. Are we including children with special needs and behavioral challenges?
3. What does true inclusion look like in our programming?
4. How can we advocate for children on the margins?
5. Do we see potential in every child—even the "difficult" ones?

Chapter 15: Lead by Example

1. Am I living out the values I want our kids to adopt?
2. What do my habits teach the children who are watching me?
3. How is my character shaping the culture of our ministry?
4. In what areas do I need to grow as a role model?
5. Do our volunteers know that their lives preach louder than their lessons?

Chapter 16: Scripture is Foundational

1. How much Scripture are our kids hearing, memorizing, and applying?
2. Do we help children connect the Bible to real life?
3. Are our lessons more opinion-based or Scripture-based?
4. What Bible tools or resources could we put in kids' hands?
5. How can we encourage families to read the Bible together?

Chapter 17: Witnesses for God in Youth

1. How are we training kids to stand for their faith in today's world?
2. Are we challenging older kids to take ownership of their beliefs?
3. What does it look like to be a young witness for Christ?
4. Are we helping kids develop a biblical worldview?
5. How can we better support spiritual boldness in children?

Chapter 18: Early Faith and Godly Homes

1. What are we doing to nurture spiritual maturity in kids—early?
2. How can we partner with parents to build godly homes?
3. Do we affirm kids who take their faith seriously?
4. Are we helping kids make faith their own—not just their parents'?
5. What role does family play in a child's spiritual formation?

Chapter 19: Long-Term Faithfulness

1. Are we helping children build a faith that lasts?
2. What systems do we have in place for long-term discipleship?
3. How can we celebrate spiritual "anniversaries" and growth?
4. Are we tracking where our kids go spiritually after they leave our ministry?
5. What legacy are we helping children build?

Chapter 20: Don't Miss the "Some Good Thing"

1. Is there a struggling child in our ministry who needs special attention?
2. What strengths might be hiding behind a child's behavior?
3. Are we mentoring any kids who show spiritual potential?
4. Who is God asking me to look at differently this week?
5. Do we truly believe that every child has "some good thing" within them?

Chapter 21: The Quiet Ones Count Too

1. Are we noticing the quiet, obedient, faithful kids—or only the loud ones?
2. What roles can introverted kids play in the life of the church?
3. How do we affirm children who serve in small but meaningful ways?
4. Are we giving equal platform to kids with different personalities and abilities?
5. Do we celebrate character as much as charisma?

Chapter 22–23: Faith in the Face of Loss

1. How do we support children and families walking through grief?
2. Are we modeling faith and trust in hard seasons?
3. What lessons of hope and resurrection are we teaching?
4. How can we remind kids that God is close—even in heartbreak?
5. Are we making space for lament, prayer, and healing in our ministry?

These 110 questions aren't meant to overwhelm you—but to inspire reflection, conversation, and growth. Think of them as a tool to help you slow down, take inventory, and listen for God's direction as you continue serving the next generation. You might choose to walk through one chapter per week as a team, allowing space for honest discussion, encouragement, and shared insight. Or maybe you'll use them personally—highlighting what's going well in your ministry and circling back to areas that need fresh vision or improvement.

However you decide to engage with these questions, remember this: reflection leads to transformation. When we make time to evaluate where we are, we position ourselves to grow into who God is calling us to become. The goal is not perfection—it's faithfulness. And Jesus honors every effort you make to love, teach, and disciple His little ones well.

So take your time. Pray through the hard questions. Celebrate the progress you've made. And stay committed to the journey. May this final chapter be more than a conclusion—may it be a launchpad toward deeper impact, stronger teams, healthier leadership, and a renewed passion to serve children more faithfully, more intentionally, and more like Jesus. You've got this—and we're cheering you on.

About the Author

Ryan Frank is a pastor, author, entrepreneur, and passionate advocate for those serving the next generation. As the co-founder of KidzMatter, Ryan has spent more than 30 years equipping and encouraging children's ministry leaders around the world. His deep love for the Church and unwavering belief in the importance of discipling kids have shaped everything he does—from conferences and training programs to publishing resources and mentoring ministry leaders.

Ryan and his wife Beth are the publishers of KidzMatter Magazine, founders of KidMin Academy, and hosts of the annual KidzMatter Conference, now the largest gathering of children's ministry leaders in the United States. Ryan is also the author of over 10 books, including *The KidzMatter Playbook*, *Ten Sentences to Revolutionize Your Ministry*, and *Eat the Frog First*.

Ryan holds a Master's degree in Bible and lives in Indiana with Beth and their three daughters, Luci, Londyn, and Lily. Together, Ryan and Beth lead KidzMatter with a shared passion: to serve those who serve kids. Whether speaking on stage or encouraging leaders one-on-one, Ryan's mission is simple—help others win in ministry and in life.

When he's not coaching ministry leaders or creating resources, Ryan enjoys spending time in the backyard with his Blackstone grill, traveling with Beth, or discovering new ways to use AI in both life and ministry.

You can connect with Ryan at www.kidzmatter.com or by email at ryan@kidzmatter.com.